Descendants of Henry William Tucker

Generation 1

1. **HENRY WILLIAM[1] TUCKER** was born on 27 Sep 1791 in Maryland. He died on 28 Jun 1863 in Carroll County, Ohio. He married (1) **ANNA ROBY** on 10 Sep 1826 in Tuscarawas County, Ohio. She died before 10 Sep 1848. He married (2) **TELITHA SPENCER** on 10 Sep 1848 in Leesburgh, Carroll County, Ohio. She was born about 1826 in Virginia. He married **SARAH TUCKER**. She was born in Maryland. She died on 23 Dec 1822.

More About Henry William Tucker:
Burial: Leesville Cemetery, Leesville, Carroll County, Ohio
Living In: 1850 Orange Township, Carroll County, Ohio
Living In: 1860 Orange Township, Carroll County, Ohio
Military Service: War of 1812; Sergeant, Captain Cox's Company, Maryland Militia

Notes for Henry William Tucker:
Listed in Carroll County, Ohio records as a veteran of the War of 1812.

Birthdate is from headstone.

Henry William Tucker and Anna Roby had the following children:

2. i. HOLLIS[2] TUCKER was born on 25 May 1830 in Leesburg, Carroll County, Ohio. He died on 28 Mar 1897 in Holton, Kansas. He married Sarah Ann McKeever, daughter of Clark McKeever and Jane Wallace on 20 Oct 1853 in Hocking County, Ohio. She was born on 20 Oct 1832 in Chester County, Pennsylvania. She died in 1909 in Holton, Kansas.

    ii. W. L. TUCKER was born about 1831.

3. iii. WESLEY SUMMERS TUCKER was born on 03 Apr 1834 in Leesburg, Carroll County, Ohio. He died on 14 Aug 1906 in Goodhope Township, Hocking County, Ohio. He married Phebe Hutson, daughter of James Hutson and Ellenor Clark on 01 May 1856 in Hocking County, Ohio. She was born on 18 May 1834 in Carroll County, Ohio. She died on 18 Nov 1905 in Lancaster, Ohio.

4. iv. WILLIAM HENRY HARRISON TUCKER was born on 08 May 1840 in Leesburg, Carroll County, Ohio. He died on 16 Feb 1904 in Bartlett Township, Todd County, Minnesota. He married Rebecca J. Russell, daughter of Samuel Russell and Caroline (unknown) on 07 Jul 1864 in Hocking County, Ohio. She was born on 18 Jul 1843 in Knox County, Ohio. She died on 28 Jan 1890.

More About Telitha Spencer:
Living In: 1880 in With Francis, Charles and Amos in Leesburgh, Carroll County, Ohio.

Henry William Tucker and Telitha Spencer had the following children:

5. v. FRANCIS MARION TUCKER was born in Jul 1855 in Carroll County, Ohio. He died in 1923 in Colorado. He married Anna Elizabeth Wallace, daughter of Sylvester Wallace and Jane Brann on 18 Apr 1881 in Carroll County, Ohio. She was born on 10 Sep 1856 in Hagerstown, Ohio. She died on 22 Apr 1938 in Goshen Township, Tuscarawas County, Ohio.

    vi. CHARLES CARROLL TUCKER was born on 01 Jun 1858 in Carroll County, Ohio. He married (1) LULU REA on 25 Oct 1882 in Carroll County, Ohio. She was born in Sep 1864 in Ohio. He married (2) IDA M. FISHER, daughter of James Fisher and Nancy

Stevens on 24 Jan 1912 in Franklin County, Ohio. She was born on 06 Jan 1860 in Warfield, Ohio.

More About Charles Carroll Tucker:
Living In: 1880 With his mother in Leesburgh, Carroll County, Ohio.
Occupation: 1880 in Leesburgh, Carroll County, Ohio; Sewing Machine Agent
Occupation: 1900 in Columbus, Franklin County, Ohio; Clerk in Dry Goods Store
Occupation: 1912 in Columbus, Franklin County, Ohio; Salesman

6. vii. AMOS CARR TUCKER was born in Nov 1861 in Carroll County, Ohio. He died after 03 Apr 1930. He married Leah Norris, daughter of David Norris and Harriet Ann Denning on 05 Mar 1885 in Tuscarawas County, Ohio. She was born about 1866 in Ohio. She died after 03 Apr 1930.

Henry William Tucker and Sarah Tucker had the following children:

7. viii. ETHELDRA ANN TUCKER was born about 1814 in Maryland. She died before 05 Oct 1855 in Ohio. She married Henry France on 08 Dec 1831 in Tuscarawas County, Ohio. He was born about 1811 in Pennsylvania. He died in 1869 in Ohio.

8. ix. CAROLINE TUCKER was born on 23 Dec 1816 in Ohio. She died on 20 Oct 1895 in New Philadelphia, Tuscarawas County, Ohio. She married Jacob B. Knisely, son of John Knisely on 16 May 1841 in Tuscarawas County, Ohio. He was born on 16 Jun 1809 in Ohio. He died on 03 Sep 1898 in Ohio.

9. x. LUCINDA TUCKER was born on 06 Jun 1820 in Leesburg, Carroll County, Ohio. She died on 03 Mar 1898 in Holton, Kansas. She married John Black, son of Andrew Black and Jane Livingston on 10 Sep 1845 in Carroll County, Ohio. He was born on 25 Apr 1817 in Washington County, Pennsylvania. He died on 22 Nov 1895 in Holton, Kansas.

10. xi. MARY E. TUCKER was born in 1822 in Carroll County, Ohio. She died on 16 Oct 1878 in Hocking County, Ohio. She married George Marshall, son of Robert Marshall and Jane Lemmon on 11 May 1843 in Carroll County, Ohio. He was born in 1818 in Ohio. He died on 20 Apr 1863 in Nashville, Tennessee.

Generation 2

2. **HOLLIS^2 TUCKER** (Henry William^1) was born on 25 May 1830 in Leesburg, Carroll County, Ohio. He died on 28 Mar 1897 in Holton, Kansas. He married Sarah Ann McKeever, daughter of Clark McKeever and Jane Wallace on 20 Oct 1853 in Hocking County, Ohio. She was born on 20 Oct 1832 in Chester County, Pennsylvania. She died in 1909 in Holton, Kansas.

More About Hollis Tucker:
Occupation: 1850 in Lee Township, Athens County, Ohio; Student
Occupation: 1870 in Holton, Jackson County, Kansas; Dry Goods Merchant
Occupation: 1880 in Franklin Township, Jackson County, Kansas; Merchant
Military Service: Bet. 05 Feb-27 Aug 1864 in Civil War; Quarter Master Sergeant, Company I, 151st Ohio Infantry, U.S. Army

Notes for Hollis Tucker:
Mustered out of 151st Ohio Infantry at Camp Chase, Columbus, Ohio.

The Holton Recorder, April 1, 1897.

Hollis Tucker, one of the most prominent business men of our city, died at his residence on west Fourth street, Sunday, March 28, 1897, aged 66 years, 10 months and 20 days. Hollis Tucker was born at Leesburg, Carrol county, Ohio, May 25, 1830. He was educated in the common schools of Ohio and at the academy of Albany, Ohio. In 1853 he married Miss Sarah A. McKeever, and in 1858 they came to Kansas, but returned to Ohio the same year. During the rebellion Mr. Tucker served in the 151st regiment, Co. I., O.V.I, as commissary sergeant. In his absence Mrs. Tucker kept the postoffice and took care of the little family. They again came to Kansas in 1865, locating in Holton in July of that year. In 1866 Mr. Tucker engaged in merchandising, which he has followed continuously to the present time. Mr. Tucker has been prominently connected with nearly every public enterprise that has benefitted and helped build up our city. In the contest of locating the county seat and building the courthouse he was one of the leaders. He perhaps did as much to secure the building of the Kansas Central railway to Holton as any other single man, and his labor and zeal was not less effectual in securing the Rock Island and Northwestern railroads. In building up Campbell University he has from the first stood shoulder to shoulder with the leaders of that enterprise, and for the past ten years has served as the president of the board of directors of that institution. Some four years ago on the death of County Treasurer George Lowell, Mr. Tucker was appointed to the office, and at the next general election he was elected to serve out Mr. Lowell's unexpired term, and also for a new term of two years, and it is generally conceded that the county never had a more competent, honest and faithful official .... When his country needed his services as a soldier he left his store and post office to the care of his wife and went to the front as a private in the ranks. He leaves his wife and seven children living, H. C. Tucker, Miss Mary Rose, Misses Florence and Clara, of this place; Mack, in the employ of the Rock Island at Clyde; Sherd, train dispatcher on the Northwestern, and Will, engaged in mining in Colorado .

Personal. A. M. Tucker, of Clifton, Kan., and Sherd Tucker, of Kansas City, were called home the first of the week by the death of their father. The Holton Recorder, April 1, 1897.

More About Sarah Ann McKeever:
Living In: 1900 Holton, Jackson County, Kansas

Notes for Sarah Ann McKeever:
Obituary published in "The Holton Recorder" in Holton, Kansas on December 2, 1909.

Hollis Tucker and Sarah Ann McKeever had the following children:

     i. HENRY CLARK[3] TUCKER was born on 28 Sep 1855 in Hocking County, Ohio. He died on 26 Jun 1921 in Kansas City, Jackson County, Missouri. He married Jean E. Harding on 22 Sep 1886 in Valley Falls, Jackson County, Kansas. She was born in Mar 1867 in Pennsylvania.

     More About Henry Clark Tucker:
     Burial: 28 Jun 1921 in Holton, Kansas
     Living In: 1921 Holton, Jackson County, Kansas
     Occupation: 1900 in Holton, Jackson County, Kansas; Dealer in Boots and Shoes
     Occupation: 1910 in Holton, Jackson County, Kansas; Retired
     Occupation: 1920 in Kansas City, Jackson County, Missouri; None

    ii. WILLIAM A. TUCKER was born on 01 Sep 1859 in Hocking County, Ohio. He died on 28 Mar 1926 in Kansas City, Missouri.

     More About William A. Tucker:
     Occupation: 1900 in Pendleton Township, St. Francois County, Missouri; Baggage Man
     Occupation: 1920 in Kansas City, Jackson County, Missouri; None

11.   iii.   MARY LINCOLN TUCKER was born on 28 Jan 1861 in Gibisonville, Ohio. She died on 20 Jun 1931 in Kansas City, Jackson County, Missouri. She married Charles E. Rose on 12 May 1885 in Holton, Jackson County, Kansas. He was born in May 1860 in Kansas. He died between 18 Apr 1910-05 Jan 1920.

12.   iv.   ANGUS MCIVOR TUCKER was born on 01 Oct 1862 in Gibisonville, Ohio. He died on 30 Oct 1943 in Topeka, Kansas. He married Edith Idella McKee, daughter of Abraham McKee and Martha Anne Armstrong on 28 Dec 1887 in Havensville, Kansas. She was born in Apr 1868 in Kansas. She died in 1958.

        v.   FLORENCE KATHERINE TUCKER was born in Sep 1868 in Holton, Kansas. She died on 15 Aug 1948 in Kansas City, Missouri.

                More About Florence Katherine Tucker:
                Living In: 1900 With her mother in Holton, Jackson County, Kansas
                Living In: 1910 With her sister, Clara, and her family in Kansas City, Jackson County, Missouri.
                Occupation: 1900 Holton, Jackson County, Kansas; Clerk
                Occupation: 1920 Franklin, Jackson County, Kansas; Probate Judge Clerk

        vi.   PHILLIP SHERIDAN TUCKER was born on 19 Jan 1870 in Holton, Kansas. He died on 12 Dec 1937 in Kansas City, Jackson County, Missouri.

                More About Phillip Sheridan Tucker:
                Burial: 14 Dec 1937 in Penwell-Gabel Cemetery and Mausoleum, Topeka, Shawnee County, Kansas
                Occupation: 1900 in Kansas City, Wyandotte County, Kansas; Train Dispatcher
                Occupation: 1910 in Kansas City, Jackson County, Missouri; Railroad Train Dispatcher
                Occupation: 1930 in Kansas City, Jackson County, Missouri; None

                Notes for Phillip Sheridan Tucker:
                Death certificate states he was single.
                ----

13.   vii.   CLARA BELLE TUCKER was born on 20 Apr 1876 in Holton, Jackson County, Kansas. She died on 01 Jun 1951 in Kansas City, Jackson County, Missouri. She married George Gilchrist Moore on 28 Sep 1898 in Holton, Jackson County, Kansas. He was born on 19 Jul 1876 in Holton, Jackson County, Kansas.

3. **WESLEY SUMMERS^2 TUCKER** (Henry William^1) was born on 03 Apr 1834 in Leesburg, Carroll County, Ohio. He died on 14 Aug 1906 in Goodhope Township, Hocking County, Ohio. He married Phebe Hutson, daughter of James Hutson and Ellenor Clark on 01 May 1856 in Hocking County, Ohio. She was born on 18 May 1834 in Carroll County, Ohio. She died on 18 Nov 1905 in Lancaster, Ohio.

More About Wesley Summers Tucker:
Burial: Fairview Methodist Church Cemetery, Good Hope Township, Hocking County, Ohio
Living In: 1850 With his half sister, Etheldra, and her family in Dover Township, Tuscarawas County, Ohio.
Living In: 1890 Goodhope Township, Hocking County, Ohio
Occupation: 1850 in Dover Township, Tuscarawas County, Ohio; Chair Maker

Occupation: 1860 in New Lexington, Perry County, Ohio; Carpenter
Occupation: 1870 in Laurel Township, Hocking County, Ohio; Cabinet Maker
Occupation: 1880 in Laurel Township, Hocking County, Ohio; Working on Saw Mill
Occupation: 1900 in Rockbridge, Good Hope Township, Hocking County, Ohio; Proprietor
of Planning Mill
Military Service: Bet. 04 Aug 1861-16 Aug 1863 ; Company B, 31st Ohio Infantry, U.S.
Army Property: 1870 in Laurel Township, Hocking County, Ohio; 25 acres Improved and
18 Acres Unimproved

Notes for Wesley Summers Tucker:
Mustered out of the U.S. Army at Camp Thomas, near Columbus, Ohio.

Registered for draft June 1863 in Laurel Township, Hocking County, Ohio.

More About Phebe Hutson:
Burial: Fairview Methodist Church Cemetery, Good Hope Township, Hocking County, Ohio

Notes for Phebe Hutson:
Ohio death index gives birth year as 1834. 1900 U.S. census gives birth date as May
1834. Headstone gives birth year as 1834.

First name is from her headstone.

Wesley Summers Tucker and Phebe Hutson had the following children:

14.   i. JOSEPH B.[3] TUCKER was born on 02 Feb 1857 in Hocking County, Ohio. He died on 13
Jun 1926 in Columbus, Franklin County, Ohio. He married Nellie May Blackburn,
daughter of William Blackburn and Hannah McGraco on 23 Dec 1880 in Hocking
County, Ohio. She was born on 15 Aug 1858 in Pickaway County, Ohio. She died on
06 Nov 1935 in Columbus, Franklin County, Ohio.

15.   ii. HOLLIS CLARK TUCKER was born on 15 Aug 1858 in Hocking County, Ohio. He died on 25
Apr 1916 in Columbus, Franklin County, Ohio. He married (1) CLARA FOX, daughter of
Peter Fox and Deborah White on 16 Feb 1879 in Hocking County, Ohio. She was born
on 27 Sep 1857 in Laurel Township, Hocking County, Ohio. She died on 30 Dec 1923
in Laurelville, Hocking County, Ohio. He married (2) ELIZA LUCRETIA HULS, daughter of
David William Huls and Eliza Ann Peters on 12 Jul 1893 in Hocking County, Ohio. She
was born on 19 Jan 1875 in Hocking County, Ohio. She died on 21 Nov 1960 in
Hocking County, Ohio.

      iii. SARAH SARVILLA TUCKER was born on 20 May 1860 in New Lexington, Perry County,
Ohio. She died on 04 Jun 1871 in Laurel Township, Hocking County, Ohio.

      iv. BETTY EMMA TUCKER was born on 17 Feb 1862 in Ohio. She died on 01 Oct 1863
in Ohio.

      v. ELLA SOMORRAH TUCKER was born on 09 Mar 1866 in Ohio. She died on 21 Aug
1885 in Tennessee.

      More About Ella Somorrah Tucker:
      Burial: Mount Ararat Cemetery, Lawrence County, Tennessee

vi. JAMES HENRY TUCKER was born on 25 Apr 1873 in Laurel Township, Hocking County, Ohio. He died on 27 Feb 1878 in Laurel Township, Hocking County, Ohio.

4. **WILLIAM HENRY HARRISON[2] TUCKER** (Henry William[1]) was born on 08 May 1840 in Leesburg, Carroll County, Ohio. He died on 16 Feb 1904 in Bartlett Township, Todd County, Minnesota. He married Rebecca J. Russell, daughter of Samuel Russell and Caroline (unknown) on 07 Jul 1864 in Hocking County, Ohio. She was born on 18 Jul 1843 in Knox County, Ohio. She died on 28 Jan 1890.

More About William Henry Harrison Tucker:
Burial: Greenlawn Cemetery, Verndale, Wadena County, Minnesota
Living In: 1875 Martinsburg, Knox County, Ohio
Living In: 1900 With his daughter, Constance, and her family in Bartlett Township, Todd County, Minnesota.
Occupation: 1860 in Orange Township, Carroll County, Ohio; Chair Maker
Occupation: 1870 in Bladensburg, Jackson Township, Knox County, Ohio; Painting
Occupation: 1880 in Pleasant Township, Knox County, Ohio; General Merchandise
Occupation: Chair Maker, Brick Layer, Merchant
Military Service: Bet. 12 Oct 1861-May 1864 in Civil War; Company K, 51st Ohio Infantry, U.S. Army

More About Rebecca J. Russell:
Burial: Greenlawn Cemetery, Verndale, Wadena County, Minnesota

William Henry Harrison Tucker and Rebecca J. Russell had the following children:

i. WILLIAM R.[3] TUCKER was born on 07 May 1865 in ohio. He died on 24 May 1944. He married Augusta M. Kruger, daughter of John Kruger and Louisa Greiger about 1907. She was born on 22 Nov 1869 in Germany. She died on 06 Aug 1959 in Los Angeles County, California.

More About William R. Tucker:
Burial: Riverside Cemetery, Fargo, Cass County, North Dakota
Occupation: 1905 in Moorhead, Clay County, Minnesota; Bookkeeper
Occupation: 1910 in Fargo, Cass County, North Dakota; Real Estate
Occupation: 1920 in Fargo, Cass County, North Dakota; County Auditor
Occupation: 1930 in Fargo, Cass County, North Dakota; Accountant
Military Service: Bet. 23 Jun 1898-18 Apr 1899 in Second Lieutenant; Company A, 1st Texas Infantry, U.S. Army

17. ii. OLIVER R. TUCKER was born on 13 Dec 1866 in Ohio. He died on 04 Feb 1905 in Cass County, North Dakota. He married Augusta M. Kruger, daughter of John Kruger and Louisa Greiger on 24 Jul 1895 in West Superior, Douglas County, Wisconsin. She was born on 22 Nov 1869 in Germany. She died on 06 Aug 1959 in Los Angeles County, California.

iii. SAMUEL L. TUCKER was born on 07 Mar 1870 in Jackson Township, Knox County, Ohio.

17. iv. CONSTANCE CAROLINE TUCKER was born on 17 Apr 1873 in Ohio. She died on 14 Dec 1962 in Koochiching County, Minnesota. She married FRANK WYMAN FOSTER. He was born in Dec 1863 in Wisconsin. He died on 25 Feb 1941 in Koochiching County, Minnesota.

v. MARY JANE TUCKER was born on 24 Jul 1875 in Martinsburg, Knox County, Ohio.

She died on 18 Feb 1893.

More About Mary Jane Tucker:
Burial: Greenlawn Cemetery, Verndale, Wadena County, Minnesota

vi.   CARY HENRY TUCKER was born on 24 Jul 1875 in Martinsburg, Knox County, Ohio. He died on 18 Apr 1952 in Staples, Todd county, Minnesota. He married SARAH ROBERTSON. She was born about 1858 in Iowa. She died on 27 Feb 1931 in Wadena County, Minnesota.

More About Cary Henry Tucker:
Burial: Greenlawn Cemetery, Verndale, Wadena County, Minnesota
Living In: 1910 Dilworth, Clay County, Minnesota
Occupation: 1900 in Bartlett Township, Todd County, Minnesota; Farmer
Occupation: 1920 in Verndale, Wadena County, Minnesota; House Carpenter
Occupation: 1930 in Verndale, Wadena County, Minnesota; Odd Jobs Laborer

18.   vii.   CHARLES WESLEY TUCKER was born on 05 May 1878 in Martinsburg, Knox County, Ohio. He died on 14 Sep 1949 in St. Paul, Ramsey County, Minnesota. He married Mary Karen Sorenson, daughter of Rasmus Sorenson between 05 Jun 1900-13 Jun 1905. She was born about 1882 in Minnesota. She died on 03 Jan 1950 in Bemidji, Beltrami County, Minnesota.

5.   FRANCIS MARION^2 TUCKER (Henry William^1) was born in Jul 1855 in Carroll County, Ohio. He died in 1923 in Colorado. He married Anna Elizabeth Wallace, daughter of Sylvester Wallace and Jane Brann on 18 Apr 1881 in Carroll County, Ohio. She was born on 10 Sep 1856 in Hagerstown, Ohio. She died on 22 Apr 1938 in Goshen Township, Tuscarawas County, Ohio.

More About Francis Marion Tucker:
Living In: 1880 With his mother in Leesburgh, Carroll County, Ohio.
Occupation: 1880 in Leesburgh, Carroll County, Ohio; Brick Moulder
Occupation: 1900 in New Philadelphia, Tuscarawas County, Ohio; Brick Mason
Occupation: 1910 in Denver, Denver County, Colorado; Brick Mason
Occupation: 1920 in Denver, Denver County, Colorado; Brick Mason

More About Anna Elizabeth Wallace:
Burial: 25 Apr 1938 in East Avenue Cemetery
Occupation: 1930 in Franktown, Douglas County, Colorado; Housekeeper

Francis Marion Tucker and Anna Elizabeth Wallace had the following children:

i.   ARTHUR WALLACE^3 TUCKER was born on 24 Feb 1882 in Orange Township, Carroll County, Ohio. He died on 07 Oct 1961 in Houston, Harris County, Texas.

More About Arthur Wallace Tucker:
Burial: Rosehill Cemetery, Tulsa, Oklahoma
Occupation: 1900 in New Philadelphia, Tuscarawas County, Ohio; Day Laborer

ii.   JOHN FOREST TUCKER was born on 28 Aug 1883 in Ohio. He died on 12 May 1963 in Tuscarawas County, Ohio.

iii.

More About John Forest Tucker:

Living In: 1963 New Philadelphia, Tuscarawas County, Ohio
Occupation: 1900 in New Philadelphia, Tuscarawas County, Ohio; Printing
Office Compositor

iii. MABEL J. TUCKER was born in Jan 1887 in Ohio.

More About Mabel J. Tucker:
Living In: 1910 With her parents in Denver, Denver County, Colorado.

6. **AMOS CARR**[2] **TUCKER** (Henry William[1]) was born in Nov 1861 in Carroll County, Ohio. He died after 3 Apr 1930. He married Leah Norris, daughter of David Norris and Harriet Ann Denning on 05 Mar 1885 in Tuscarawas County, Ohio. She was born about 1866 in Ohio. She died after 03 Apr 1930.

More About Amos Carr Tucker:
Living In: 1920 San Jose, Santa Clara County, California
Living In: 1930 San Jose, Santa Clara County, California
Occupation: 1910 in Conneaut, Ashtabula County, Ohio; Popcorn Vender

Amos Carr Tucker and Leah Norris had the following children:

i. CHARLES ELMER[3] TUCKER was born on 29 Aug 1885 in Ohio. He died on 06 Oct 1956 in Santa Clara County, California. He married INA R. (UNKNOWN).

More About Charles Elmer Tucker:
Occupation: 1918 in San Miguel, San Luis Obispo County, California; Mechanic

ii. HOWARD CARROLL TUCKER was born on 22 Jun 1889 in Newcomerstown, Tuscarawas County, Ohio. He died on 23 Dec 1952 in Conneaut, Ashtabula County, Ohio.

More About Howard Carroll Tucker:
Burial: 27 Dec 1952 in East Lake Cemetery, North Kingsville, Ohio
Occupation: Barber

iii. HAZEL TUCKER was born on 07 Apr 1891 in Ohio. She died on 14 Jun 1956 in Santa Clara County, California. She married (1) STANLEY ABBOT JOHNS, son of John Robert Johns and Addie Merrill on 27 Aug 1932 in Hollister, San Benito County, California. He was born about 1887. She married (UNKNOWN) HOWELL.

iv. RUTH V. TUCKER was born on 03 Jul 1893 in Newcomerstown, Tuscarawas County, Ohio. She died on 06 Jan 1983 in Santa Clara County, California. She married (UNKNOWN) SAUNDERS.

v. MARIE TUCKER was born on 03 Apr 1896 in Ohio. She died on 13 Aug 1944 in Los Angeles County, California. She married Frank N. Cochran, son of Asa H. Cochran and Lucy Such on 28 May 1917 in Los Angeles County, California. He was born about 1867.

7. **ETHELDRA ANN**[2] **TUCKER** (Henry William[1]) was born about 1814 in Maryland. She died before 05 Oct 1855 in Ohio. She married Henry France on 08 Dec 1831 in Tuscarawas County, Ohio. He was born about 1811 in Pennsylvania. He died in 1869 in Ohio.

Notes for Etheldra Ann Tucker:
Name on her marriage license is Teldoann Tucker.

First name on 1850 U.S. census is Theldriana.

More About Henry France:
Occupation: 1850 in Dover Township, Tuscarawas County, Ohio; Chair
Maker
Occupation: 1860 in Canal Dover, Tuscarawas County, Ohio; Chair Maker
Occupation: Chair and Furniture Maker

Henry France and Etheldra Ann Tucker had the following children:

    i.   SARAH CATHERINE[3] FRANCE was born about 1832 in Ohio.

    ii.   OLIVER FRANCE was born about 1836 in Ohio. He died in May 1864.

        More About Oliver France:
        Military Service: Civil War; Captain in 126th Ohio Infantry, U.S. Army

        Notes for Oliver France:
        Killed in the Battle of the Wilderness, May 1864.

    iii. LUCINDA FRANCE was born about 1839 in Ohio.

    iv. MARY FRANCE was born about 1842 in Ohio.

    v.   ELIZABETH FRANCE was born about 1846 in Ohio.

        More About Elizabeth France:
        Living In: 1870 With John Stansbery and his family in Ligonier, Noble County,
        Indiana.
        Occupation: 1870 in Ligonier, Noble County, Indiana; Telegraph Operator

    vi. WILLIAM W. FRANCE was born about 1850 in Ohio.

        More About William W. France:
        Living In: 1870 With John Stansbery and his family in Ligonier, Noble County,
        Indiana.
        Occupation: 1870 in Ligonier, Noble County, Indiana; Painter

    vii. CHARLES H. FRANCE was born about 1852 in Ohio.

        More About Charles H. France:
        Living In: 1870 With John Stansbery and his family in Ligonier, Noble County,
        Indiana.
        Occupation: 1870 in Ligonier, Noble County, Indiana; Painter

8. CAROLINE[2] TUCKER (Henry William[1]) was born on 23 Dec 1816 in Ohio. She died on 20 Oct 1895 in
New Philadelphia, Tuscarawas County, Ohio. She married Jacob B. Knisely, son of John Knisely on
16 May 1841 in Tuscarawas County, Ohio. He was born on 16 Jun 1809 in Ohio. He died on 03

Sep 1898 in Ohio.

More About Caroline Tucker:
Burial: Fair Street Cemetery, New Philadelphia, Tuscarawas County, Ohio

More About Jacob B. Knisely:
Burial: Fair Street Cemetery, New Philadelphia, Tuscarawas County, Ohio
Occupation: 1850 in New Philadelphia, Tuscarawas County, Ohio; Carpenter
Occupation: 1860 in Goshen Township, Tuscarawas County, Ohio; Carpenter
Occupation: 1870 in New Philadelphia, Tuscarawas County, Ohio; Carpenter
Occupation: 1880 in New Philadelphia, Tuscarawas County, Ohio; Carpenter

Jacob B. Knisely and Caroline Tucker had the following children:

    i.   GEORGE WASHINGTON[3] KNISELY was born about 1842 in Ohio.

    ii.   JAMES KNISELY was born about 1844 in Ohio.

    iii.   JOHN W. KNISELY was born in 1847 in Ohio. He died in 1927. He married MARY HELEN (UNKNOWN). She was born in 1853.

        More About John W. Knisely:
        Burial: Fair Street Cemetery, New Philadelphia, Tuscarawas County, Ohio
        Living In: 1870 With his parents in New Philadelphia, Tuscarawas County, Ohio.
        Occupation: 1870 in New Philadelphia, Tuscarawas County, Ohio; Carpenter

    iv.   HENRY KNISELY was born about 1849.

        More About Henry Knisely:
        Occupation: 1870 in New Philadelphia, Tuscarawas County, Ohio; Carpenter

    v.   BENJAMIN FRANKLIN KNISELY was born about 1852 in Ohio.

        More About Benjamin Franklin Knisely:
        Living In: 1880 With his parents in New Philadelphia, Tuscarawas County, Ohio.
        Occupation: 1870 in New Philadelphia, Tuscarawas County, Ohio; Works in Retail Grocery
        Occupation: 1880 in New Philadelphia, Tuscarawas County, Ohio; Carpenter

    vi.   ANNA KNISELY was born about 1857 in Ohio.

9.   LUCINDA[2] TUCKER (Henry William[1]) was born on 06 Jun 1820 in Leesburg, Carroll County, Ohio. She died on 03 Mar 1898 in Holton, Kansas. She married John Black, son of Andrew Black and Jane Livingston on 10 Sep 1845 in Carroll County, Ohio. He was born on 25 Apr 1817 in Washington County, Pennsylvania. He died on 22 Nov 1895 in Holton, Kansas.

More About Lucinda Tucker:
Burial: Holton Cemetery, Holton, Jackson County, Kansas

More About John Black:
Burial: Holton Cemetery, Holton, Jackson County, Kansas
Occupation: 1860 in Laurel Township, Hocking County, Ohio; Farmer

Occupation: 1870 in Franklin Township, Jackson County, Kansas; Farmer
Occupation: 1880 in Liberty Township, Jackson County, Kansas; Farmer

Notes for John Black:

The Holton Recorder, November 28,
1895.
John Black was born in Washington county, Pennsylvania, April 25, 1817, and died at his home in this city, November 22, 1895, aged 78 years, six months and 27 days. In the year 1830, when thirteen years of age, he removed with his parents to Carroll county, Ohio, where fifteen years later he was married united in marriage to Miss Lucinda Tucker, with whom he lived, lacking only a few days of fifty years. In .1850 they moved to Hocking county, Ohio, and from there to Jackson county, Kansas, in 1866, where they have since resided, Mr. Black was converted and joined the Methodist church in 1840, and has been a devoted, zealous working member of the same for over half a century. For twenty-six years, sixteen in Ohio and ten in Kansas, he was a class leader ....
He leaves an aged widow and three sons, Samuel T, A. H, and N. H. Black. Three daughters born to them preceded their father to the spirit land. The aged wife has for some time been confined to her bed, and the probabilities are that this separation will not be for long. The Holton Recorder, November 28, 1895.

John Black and Lucinda Tucker had the following children:

 i. ANDREW HENRY[3] BLACK was born on 23 May 1847 in Ohio. He died on 16 Jan 1909 in Kansas. He married MARGARET J. (UNKNOWN). She was born on 08 Dec 1845. She died on 30 Aug 1916 in Kansas.

  More About Andrew Henry Black:
  Burial: Cedar Cemetery, Cedar, Smith County, Kansas
  Living In: 1880 With his parents in Liberty Township, Jackson County, Kansas
  Occupation: 1880 in Liberty Township, Jackson County, Kansas; Salesman

 ii. SAMUEL T. BLACK was born in 1850 in Ohio. He died in 1931.

  More About Samuel T. Black:
  Burial: Holton Cemetery, Holton, Jackson County, Kansas
  Living In: 1880 With his parents in Liberty Township, Jackson County, Kansas
  Occupation: 1880 in Liberty Township, Jackson County, Kansas; Salesman

 iii. WILLIAM H. BLACK was born in 1860 in Ohio. He died in 1939. He married MARY J. PIERCE. She was born in 1856. She died in 1936.

  More About William H. Black:
  Burial: Holton Cemetery, Holton, Jackson County, Kansas
  Occupation: 1880 in Liberty Township, Jackson County, Kansas; Farmer

 iv. MARTHA JANE BLACK was born in 1862 in Ohio. She died on 23 Aug 1885.

  More About Martha Jane Black:
  Burial: Holton Cemetery, Holton, Jackson County, Kansas

10. MARY E.[2] TUCKER (Henry William[1]) was born in 1822 in Carroll County, Ohio. She died on 16 Oct

1878 in Hocking County, Ohio. She married George Marshall, son of Robert Marshall and Jane Lemmon on 11 May 1843 in Carroll County, Ohio. He was born in 1818 in Ohio. He died on 20 Apr 1863 in Nashville, Tennessee.

More About Mary E. Tucker:
Burial: Bethany Cemetery, Perry Township, Hocking County, Ohio
Living In: 1870 With Sarah, Lemon, Naomi, Joseph and James in Perry Township, Hocking County, Ohio.

More About George Marshall:
Occupation: 1860 in Laurel Township, Hocking County, Ohio; Farmer
Military Service: Bet. 01 Sep 1862-20 Apr 1863 ; Company B, 31st Ohio Infantry, U.S. Army

George Marshall and Mary E. Tucker had the following children:

    i.   SARAH J.^{3} MARSHALL was born about 1844 in Ohio.

    ii.   ROBERT H. MARSHALL was born about 1846 in Ohio.

    iii.   MARGARET MARSHALL was born in 1848 in Ohio.

    iv.   LEMON MARSHALL was born on 11 Jun 1851 in Hocking County, Ohio. He died on 31 May 1920 in Lancaster, Fairfield County, Ohio.

        More About Lemon Marshall:
        Burial: 03 Jun 1920 in Bethany Cemetery, Perry Township, Hocking County, Ohio

    v.   NAOMI MARSHALL was born in 1854 in Ohio. She married OLIVER KANE.

        More About Naomi Marshall:
        Burial: Bethany Cemetery, Perry Township, Hocking County, Ohio

    vi.   JOSEPH MARSHALL was born on 12 Apr 1857 in Ohio. He died on 15 Dec 1918 in Violet Township, Fairfield County, Ohio. He married Eliza Jane Chambers on 23 Dec 1880 in Hocking County, Ohio. She was born about 1857 in Stoutesville, Fairfield County, Ohio. She died on 09 Feb 1897 in Stoutesville, Fairfield County, Ohio.

        More About Joseph Marshall:
        Burial: 18 Dec 1918 in Bethany Cemetery, Perry Township, Hocking County, Ohio
        Occupation: 1918 in Violet Township, Fairfield County, Ohio; Farmer

    vii.   JAMES MARSHALL was born about 1862 in Ohio.

Generation 3

11.   **MARY LINCOLN^3 TUCKER** (Hollis^2, Henry William^1) was born on 28 Jan 1861 in Gibisonville, Ohio. She died on 20 Jun 1931 in Kansas City, Jackson County, Missouri. She married Charles E. Rose on 12 May 1885 in Holton, Jackson County, Kansas. He was born in May 1860 in Kansas. He died between 18 Apr 1910-05 Jan 1920.

More About Mary Lincoln Tucker:

Burial: 21 Jun 1931 in Holton Cemetery, Holton, Jackson County, Kansas
Living In: 1920 In a rooming house with daughters, Lila and Florence, in Greeley, Weld County, Colorado.
Living In: 1930 With her daughter, Lila, in Oshkosh, Winnebago County, Wisconsin
Occupation: 1880 in Franklin Township, Jackson County, Ohio; Music Teacher

More About Charles E. Rose:
Occupation: 1900 in Holton, Jackson County, Kansas; Druggist
Occupation: 1910 in Holton, Jackson County, Kansas; Insurance Agent

Charles E. Rose and Mary Lincoln Tucker had the following children:

    i.   LILA M.[4] ROSE was born in Apr 1886 in Kansas.

        More About Lila M. Rose:
        Living In: 1910 With her parents in Holton, Jackson County, Kansas.
        Living In: 1920 In a rooming house with her mother and sister, Florence, in Greeley, Weld County, Colorado.
        Living In: 1930 With her mother in Oshkosh, Winnebago County, Wisconsin.
        Occupation: 1910 in Holton, Jackson County, Kansas; School Music Teacher
        Occupation: 1920 in Greeley, Weld County, Colorado; Teacher
        Occupation: 1930 in Oshkosh, Winnebago County, Wisconsin; Teacher in Male Teachers College

    ii.   DONNA C. ROSE was born in Jan 1888 in Kansas.

        More About Donna C. Rose:
        Living In: 1910 With her parents in Holton, Jackson County, Kansas.
        Occupation: 1910 in Holton, Jackson County, Kansas; School Teacher

    iii.   FLORENCE ROSE was born in Nov 1891 in Kansas.

        More About Florence Rose:
        Living In: 1920 In a rooming house with her mother and sister, Lila, in Greeley, Weld County, Colorado.
        Occupation: 1920 in Greeley, Weld County, Colorado; Teacher

    iv.   HAROLD ROSE was born in May 1893 in Kansas.

12.   **ANGUS MCIVOR**[3] **TUCKER** (Hollis[2], Henry William[1]) was born on 01 Oct 1862 in Gibisonville, Ohio. He died on 30 Oct 1943 in Topeka, Kansas. He married Edith Idella McKee, daughter of Abraham McKee and Martha Anne Armstrong on 28 Dec 1887 in Havensville, Kansas. She was born in Apr 1868 in Kansas. She died in 1958.

More About Angus McIvor Tucker:
Burial: Penwell-Gabel Cemetery and Mausoleum, Topeka, Shawnee County, Kansas
Occupation: 1880 in Franklin Township, Jackson County, Kansas; Brick Maker
Occupation: 1900 in Clifton, Washington County, Kansas; Railroad Agent
Occupation: 1910 in Manhattan, Riley County, Kansas; Railroad Station Agent
Occupation: 1920 in Topeka Township, Shawnee County, Kansas; Chemical Office Freight
Occupation: 1930 in Topeka, Shawnee County, Kansas; Claim Adjuster for Steam Railway
Occupation: 1940 in Topeka, Shawnee County, Kansas; Retired

More About Edith Idella McKee:
Burial: Penwell-Gabel Cemetery and Mausoleum, Topeka, Shawnee County, Kansas

Angus McIvor Tucker and Edith Idella McKee had the following children:

i. CLAUDE HOLLIS[4] TUCKER was born in Oct 1888 in Onaga, Kansas. He died on 29 Oct 1949 in Norton, Kansas. He married Lura Isabel Clay, daughter of Davy Thaddeus Clay and Margaret Mitchell Cork on 22 Oct 1921 in Larned, Kansas. She was born on 01 Sep 1897 in Marshall, Kansas. She died on 04 Jun 1987 in Topeka, Kansas.

More About Claude Hollis Tucker:
Living In: 1920 With his parents in Topeka, Shawnee County, Kansas.
Occupation: 1920 in Topeka Township, Shawnee County, Kansas; Oil Lease Salesman

ii. LLOYD M. TUCKER was born on 01 Sep 1890 in Holton, Kansas. He died on 22 Dec 1964 in Topeka, Kansas. He married Bertha Mabel Worthing, daughter of Edwin Augustine Worthing and Lettie H. Moore on 17 Nov 1910 in Belvue, Kansas. She was born in 1890 in Fort Scott, Kansas. She died on 29 Jan 1984 in Oklahoma City, Oklahoma.

More About Lloyd M. Tucker:
Occupation: 1910 in Manhattan, Riley County, Texas; Railroad Telegrapher

iii. KATHERINE ANN TUCKER was born on 05 Jun 1892 in Holton, Kansas. She died on 29 Nov 1958 in Topeka, Kansas.

More About Katherine Ann Tucker:
Living In: 1920 With her parents in Topeka Township, Shawnee County, Kansas.
Living In: 1930 With her parents in Topeka, Shawnee County, Kansas.
Living In: 1940 With her parents in Topeka, Shawnee County, Kansas.
Occupation: 1920 in Topeka Township, Shawnee County, Kansas; Public School Teacher
Occupation: 1930 in Topeka, Shawnee County, Kansas; Public School Teacher
Occupation: 1940 in Topeka, Shawnee County, Kansas; Public School Teacher

iv. RAYMOND ANGUS TUCKER was born on 16 Jan 1900 in Clifton, Kansas. He died on 08 Feb 1975 in Topeka, Kansas. He married (1) RUTH ECHOLS in 1944 in Houston, Texas. She was born on 17 Aug 1911 in Parkdale, Arkansas. She died in 2005. He married (2) ELSIE MARGARET JORDAN, daughter of Frederick H. Jordan and Caroline C. (unknown) on 04 Nov 1927. She was born on 23 Jan 1900. She died on 24 Jun 1942 in Fremond, Nebraska.

More About Raymond Angus Tucker:
Burial: Penwel-Gabel Cemetery and Mausoleum, Topeka, Shawnee County, Kansas
Living In: 1930 With his parents in Topeka, Shawnee County, Kansas.
Occupation: 1920 in Topeka Township, Shawnee County, Kansas; Taxi Cab Chauffeur
Occupation: 1930 in Topeka, Shawnee County, Kansas; Used Automobile Dealer

13. **CLARA BELLE**[3] **TUCKER** (Hollis[2], Henry William[1]) was born on 20 Apr 1876 in Holton, Jackson

County, Kansas. She died on 01 Jun 1951 in Kansas City, Jackson County, Missouri. She married George Gilchrist Moore on 28 Sep 1898 in Holton, Jackson County, Kansas. He was born on 19 Jul 1876 in Holton, Jackson County, Kansas.

More About Clara Belle Tucker:
Burial: 04 Jun 1951 in Forest Hill Cemetery, Kansas City, Missouri

More About George Gilchrist Moore:
Occupation: 1900 in Ponca City, Kay County, Oklahoma Territory (present day Oklahoma); Assistant Cashier in Bank
Occupation: 1910 in Kansas City, Jackson County, Missouri; Bank Cashier
Occupation: 1918 in Kansas City, Jackson County, Missouri; Banker in New England National Bank
Occupation: 1920 in Kansas City, Jackson County, Missouri; Bank Cashier
Occupation: 1930 in Kansas City, Jackson County, Missouri; Bank Vice President
Occupation: 1940 in Kansas City, Jackson County, Missouri; Banker

George Gilchrist Moore and Clara Belle Tucker had the following child:

    i.   JAMES H.[4] MOORE was born about 1903 in Indian Territory (present day Oklahoma).

        More About James H. Moore:
        Living In: 1930 With his parents in Kansas City, Jackson County, Missouri.
        Occupation: 1930 in Kansas City, Jackson County, Missouri; Bank Cashier

14.   **JOSEPH B.[3] TUCKER** (Wesley Summers[2], Henry William[1]) was born on 02 Feb 1857 in Hocking County, Ohio. He died on 13 Jun 1926 in Columbus, Franklin County, Ohio. He married Nellie May Blackburn, daughter of William Blackburn and Hannah McGraco on 23 Dec 1880 in Hocking County, Ohio. She was born on 15 Aug 1858 in Pickaway County, Ohio. She died on 06 Nov 1935 in Columbus, Franklin County, Ohio.

More About Joseph B. Tucker:
Burial: 15 Jun 1926 in Greenlawn Cemetery, Columbus, Franklin County, Ohio
Living In: 1880 With his parents in Laurel Township, Hocking County, Ohio.
Occupation: 1870 in Laurel Township, Hocking County, Ohio; Farm Worker
Occupation: 1880 in Laurel Township, Hocking County, Ohio; Farmer
Occupation: 1900 in Lancaster, Fairfield County, Ohio; Common Labor
Occupation: 1910 in Lancaster, Fairfield County, Ohio; General Work Laborer
Occupation: 1920 in Columbus, Franklin County, Ohio; Railroad Shop Labor

More About Nellie May Blackburn:
Burial: 09 Nov 1935 in Greenlawn Cemetery, Columbus, Franklin County, Ohio
Living In: 1930 With her son, Arthur, and his family in Columbus, Franklin County, Ohio.

Notes for Nellie May Blackburn:
Ohio Marriage Records have name listed as Ellie Blackburn.

Joseph B. Tucker and Nellie May Blackburn had the following children:

    i.   NELLIE MAY[4] TUCKER was born on 22 May 1881 in Laurel Township, Hocking County, Ohio. She died on 01 Jun 1956 in Ohio. She married Fred Dennis, son of John S. Dennis and Jennie Dixie on 04 Dec 1919 in Franklin County, ohio. He was born on 14 Jul 1879 in Commercial Point, Pickaway County, Ohio. He died on 21 Dec 1959 in Columbus, Franklin County, Ohio.

More About Nellie May Tucker:
Burial: Green Lawn Cemetery, Coulumbus, Franklin County, Ohio

19.   ii. HUTSON EDWARD TUCKER was born on 15 Feb 1883 in Perry Township, Hocking County, Ohio. He died on 13 Jul 1945 in Lancaster, Fairfield County, Ohio. He married LUZELLA (ZELLA) ARTES. She was born on 10 Jan 1884 in Fairfield County, Ohio. She died on 12 Feb 1930 in Berne Township, Fairfield County, Ohio.

iii. ARTHUR LLOYD TUCKER was born on 03 Jan 1889 in Rockbridge, Hocking County, Ohio. He died on 23 Feb 1962 in Columbus, Franklin County, Ohio. He married HAZEL SIEFERT. She was born about 1891 in Ohio.

More About Arthur Lloyd Tucker:
Living In: 1920 Arthur and his family are living with his parents in Columbus, Franklin County, Ohio.
Occupation: 1920 in Columbus, Franklin County, Ohio; Painter in Couch Factory
Occupation: 1930 in Columbus, Franklin County, Ohio; Steel worker at Sanitary Works

Notes for Arthur Lloyd Tucker:
Birth date is from World War One and World War Two draft registrations.

15. **HOLLIS CLARK**[3] **TUCKER** (Wesley Summers[2], Henry William[1]) was born on 15 Aug 1858 in Hocking County, Ohio. He died on 25 Apr 1916 in Columbus, Franklin County, Ohio. He married (1) **CLARA FOX**, daughter of Peter Fox and Deborah White on 16 Feb 1879 in Hocking County, Ohio. She was born on 27 Sep 1857 in Laurel Township, Hocking County, Ohio. She died on 30 Dec 1923 in Laurelville, Hocking County, Ohio. He married (2) **ELIZA LUCRETIA HULS**, daughter of David William Huls and Eliza Ann Peters on 12 Jul 1893 in Hocking County, Ohio. She was born on 19 Jan 1875 in Hocking County, Ohio. She died on 21 Nov 1960 in Hocking County, Ohio.

More About Hollis Clark Tucker:
Burial: 28 Apr 1916 in Fairview Methodist Church Cemetery, Good Hope Township, Hocking County, Ohio
Cause Of Death: Punctured lung from fractured ribs due to being run down by a railroad train.
Occupation: 1870; Farm Worker, Laurel, Ohio
Occupation: 1900 in Rockbridge, Goodhope Township, Hocking County, Ohio; Derrick Builder
Occupation: 1910 in Goodhope Township, Hocking County, Ohio; Laborer
Occupation: Carpenter

Notes for Hollis Clark Tucker:
Death certificate gives birth date as August 15, 1854. Age given on death certificate would give a birth date of August 15, 1858. 1900 U.S. census gives birthdate as August 1858. Hollis Tucker and Clara Fox marriage license indicates an 1858 birth.

More About Clara Fox:
Burial: 01 Jan 1924 in Mount Olive Cemetery, South Perry, Hocking County, Ohio Cause Of Death: Broncial Pneumonia

Notes for Clara Fox:
1860 U.S. census has Clarissa for her first name. Her sister, Sarah, had a daughter named

Clarissa.

Hollis Clark Tucker and Clara Fox had the following children:

20.   i. CHARLES JOSEPH[4] TUCKER was born on 12 Oct 1879 in Hocking County, Ohio. He died on 13 Jan 1967 in Hocking County, Ohio. He married Beatrice Applegate, daughter of Walter Applegate and Miranda McFarland about 1903. She was born on 08 Mar 1883 in Lancaster, Ohio. She died on 13 Feb 1952 in Hocking County, Ohio.

21.   ii. MARY LOVETTA TUCKER was born on 17 Aug 1883 in Perry Township, Hocking County, Ohio. She died on 17 Feb 1951 in Salt Creek Township, Hocking County, Ohio. She married William Elmer Woltz, son of Moses H. Woltz and Anna L. Shellhammer on 14 Dec 1901 in Logan, Ohio. He was born on 30 Dec 1880 in Good Hope Township, Hocking County, Ohio. He died in 1955.

22.   iii. WILLIAM EDWARD TUCKER was born on 08 Nov 1885 in Rockbridge, Ohio. He died on 21 Apr 1975 in Plant City, Florida. He married Mary Ann Davis, daughter of Levi Davis and Mary Ann Bigham on 29 Jun 1906 in Lancaster, Ohio. She was born on 16 Mar 1887 in Laurel Township, Hocking County, Ohio. She died on 11 Mar 1971 in Lakeland, Polk County, Florida.

    iv. HARRY HERBERT TUCKER was born on 30 Oct 1887 in Good Hope Township, Hocking County, Ohio. He died on 10 Dec 1949 in Kansas. He married STELLA MAY (UNKNOWN). She was born on 20 Dec 1892 in Kansas. She died on 23 May 1980.

More About Harry Herbert Tucker:
Burial: Elim Lutheran Cemetery, Marquette, McPherson County, Kansas
Living In: 1917 Kansas City, Missouri
Living In: 1935 Denver, Denver County, Colorado
Living In: 1940 Marquette, McPherson County, Kansas
Occupation: 1917 in Oiler at Interstate Ice Company in Kansas City, Kansas
Occupation: 1920 in Denver, Denver County, Colorado; Machinist in Garage
Occupation: 1930 in Denver, Denver County, Colorado; Commercial Traveler for Farm Implements

More About Eliza Lucretia Huls:
Burial: Fairview Methodist Church Cemetery, Good Hope Township, Hocking County, Ohio
Living In: 1920 Goodhope Township, Hocking County, Ohio
Living In: 1930 Goodhope Township, Hocking County, Ohio
Living In: 1940 Rockbridge, Hocking County, Ohio

Hollis Clark Tucker and Eliza Lucretia Huls had the following children:

23.   v. DAVID WESLEY TUCKER was born on 28 Jun 1894 in Rockbridge, Hocking County, Ohio. He died on 25 Feb 1984 in Fairfield County, Ohio. He married Minnie Turner, daughter of Martin Turner and Harriet Fuller on 06 Jan 1923 in Pickaway, Ohio. She was born on 08 Jul 1901 in New Holland, Pickaway County, Ohio. She died on 16 Jan 1987 in Lancaster, Ohio.

24.   vi. BERTHA MAY TUCKER was born on 31 Mar 1896 in Millville, Hocking County, Ohio. She died on 30 Nov 1973 in Hocking County, Ohio. She married Clyde Mathias, son of William Mathias and Laura Hixon on 26 Sep 1922 in Hocking County, Ohio. He was born on 16 May 1897 in Lancaster, Ohio. He died on 05 Oct 1964 in Athens, Athens County, Ohio.

vii.   JOSEPH HULS TUCKER was born on 07 Feb 1898 in Laurel Township, Hocking County, Ohio. He died on 07 Feb 1947 in Columbus, Ohio. He married Mary Elizabeth Westenbarger, daughter of Charles Westenbarger and Florence Schultz on 20 Dec 1941 in Hocking County, Ohio. She was born on 19 Feb 1919 in Logan, Hocking County, Ohio.

More About Joseph Huls Tucker:
Burial: 10 Feb 1947 in Fairview Methodist Church Cemetery, Good Hope Township, Hocking County, Ohio
Living In: 1920 With his mother in Good Hope Township, Hocking County, Ohio.
Living In: 1930 With his mother in Good Hope Township, Hocking County, Ohio.
Living In: 1940 With his mother in Rockbridge, Hocking County, Ohio.
Occupation: 1910 in Good Hope Township, Hocking County, Ohio; Newsboy
Occupation: 1920 in Good Hope Township, Hocking County, Ohio; Restaurant Keeper
Occupation: 1930 in Good Hope Township, Hocking County, Ohio; House Painter
Occupation: 1940 in Rockbridge, Hocking County, Ohio; Highway Department Laborer
Occupation: 1941 in Rockbridge, Hocking County, Ohio; Painter

viii.   LAWRENCE MERVILL TUCKER was born on 01 May 1900 in Good Hope Township, Hocking County, Ohio. He died on 07 Mar 1903 in Goodhope Township, Hocking County, Ohio.

More About Lawrence Mervill Tucker:
Burial: Fairview Methodist Church Cemetery, Good Hope Township, Hocking County, Ohio

25.   ix. BERYL HOLLIS TUCKER was born on 19 Aug 1902 in Rockbridge, Hocking County, Ohio. He died on 11 Sep 1983 in Hocking County, Ohio. He married Ruth Irene Primmer, daughter of William Primmer and Blanche A. Starner on 01 Jan 1927 in Hocking County, Ohio. She was born on 17 Apr 1908 in Rockbridge, Hocking County, Ohio. She died on 18 Sep 2006 in Lancaster, Fairfield County, Ohio.

26.   x. NORMA IRENE TUCKER was born on 27 Mar 1905 in Rockbridge, Hocking County, Ohio. She died on 21 May 1985 in Lancaster, Fairfield County, Ohio. She married Ernest Loy Fauble, son of Chris Fauble and Eliza J. (Jennie) Dupler on 24 Dec 1926 in Hocking County, Ohio. He was born on 06 Sep 1904 in Rockbridge, Hocking County, Ohio. He died on 27 Jan 1967 in Lancaster, Fairfield County, Ohio.

xi.   DORIS ELIZA TUCKER was born on 10 Feb 1907 in Rockbridge, Good Hope Township, Hocking County, Ohio. She died on 02 Jan 1908 in Rockbridge, Good Hope Township, Hocking County, Ohio.

More About Doris Eliza Tucker:
Burial: Fairview Methodist Church Cemetery, Good Hope Township, Hocking County, Ohio

Notes for Doris Eliza Tucker:
Birth record has Dorris Eliza Tucker for name. Headstone has Doris Eliza Tucker for name.

xii. ROBERT EUGENE TUCKER was born on 04 Oct 1910 in Rockbridge, Hocking County, Ohio. He died on 13 Feb 1983 in Logan, Ohio. He married Margaret Anna Pangburn, daughter of Wesley J. Pangburn and Helen A. Stewart on 24 Oct 1952 in Fairfield County, Ohio. She was born on 13 Nov 1921 in Caribou, Maine. She died on 08 Apr 2012 in Ohio.

More About Robert Eugene Tucker:
Burial: Fairview Methodist Church Cemetery, Good Hope Township, Hocking County, Ohio
Living In: 1940 With his sister, Norma Irene, and her family in Lancaster, Fairfield County, Ohio.
Living In: 1952 Rockbridge, Hocking County, Ohio
Occupation: 1930 in Goodhope Township, Hocking County, Ohio; House Painter
Occupation: 1940 in Lancaster, Fairfield County, Ohio; Sprayer in Glass Factory
Occupation: 1952; Filling Station Operator

xiii. RUTH ESTHER TUCKER was born on 21 Feb 1913 in Rockbridge, Hocking County, Ohio. She died on 27 May 2004 in Lancaster, Fairfield County, Ohio. She married Seth William Rauch, son of William H. Rauch and Viola Mourey on 18 Oct 1941 in Perry County, Ohio. He was born on 21 Mar 1911 in Fairfield County, Ohio. He died on 13 Jan 1987 in Lancaster, Fairfield County, Ohio.

More About Ruth Esther Tucker:
Burial: Forest Rose Cemetery, Lancaster, Fairfield County, Ohio
Living In: 1941 Corning, Perry County, Ohio

xiv. FRANK K. TUCKER was born in 1915 in Ohio. He died on 12 Apr 1965 in Hocking County, Ohio.

More About Frank K. Tucker:
Burial: Fairview Methodist Church Cemetery, Good Hope Township, Hocking County, Ohio
Living In: 1940 With his mother in Rockbridge, Hocking County, Ohio.
Occupation: 1940 in Rockbridge, Hocking County, Ohio; Selector in Glass Factory Military Service: World War Two

Notes   for   Frank   K.
Tucker: Never Married.

16. OLIVER R.[3] TUCKER (William Henry Harrison[2], Henry William[1]) was born on 13 Dec 1866 in Ohio. He died on 04 Feb 1905 in Cass County, North Dakota. He married Augusta M. Kruger, daughter of John Kruger and Louisa Greiger on 24 Jul 1895 in West Superior, Douglas County, Wisconsin. She was born on 22 Nov 1869 in Germany. She died on 06 Aug 1959 in Los Angeles County, California.

More About Oliver R. Tucker:
Burial: Riverside Cemetery, Fargo, Cass County, North Dakota
Occupation: 1900 in Fargo, Cass County, North Dakota; Bookkeeper

Oliver R. Tucker and Augusta M. Kruger had the following children:

i. JOHN[4] TUCKER was born in Feb 1896 in North Dakota.

More About John Tucker:
Living In: 1910 in With his mother and step father in Fargo, Cass County, North Dakota.

    ii.   FRED TUCKER was born in Mar 1897 in North Dakota.

More About Fred Tucker:
Living In: 1910 With his mother and step father in Fargo, Cass County, North Dakota.
Living In: 1920 With his mother and step father in Fargo, Cass County, North Dakota.
Occupation: 1920 in Fargo, Cass County, North Dakota; Office Bookkeeper

17.   **CONSTANCE CAROLINE**[3] **TUCKER** (William Henry Harrison[2], Henry William[1]) was born on 17 Apr 1873 in Ohio. She died on 14 Dec 1962 in Koochiching County, Minnesota. She married **FRANK WYMAN FOSTER**. He was born in Dec 1863 in Wisconsin. He died on 25 Feb 1941 in Koochiching County, Minnesota.

More About Constance Caroline Tucker:
Occupation: 1940 in Mizpah, Koochiching County, Minnesota; Prorietor of Grocery Store

More About Frank Wyman Foster:
Occupation: 1900 in Bartlett Township, Todd County, Minnesota; Farmer
Occupation: 1905 in Bartlett Township, Todd County, Minnesota; Farmer
Occupation: 1910 in Engelwood Township, Koochiching County, Mimmesota; Feed and Hay Merchant
Occupation: 1930 in Mizpah, Koochiching County, Minnesota; General Store Merchant
Occupation: 1940 in Mizpah, Koochiching County, Minnesota; None

Frank Wyman Foster and Constance Caroline Tucker had the following children:

    i.   MARION LEROY[4] FOSTER was born on 03 Jan 1891 in Minnesota.

    ii.   ARTHUR CHRISTOPHER FOSTER was born on 06 Oct 1893 in Minnesota. He died on 18 Nov 1971 in Itaska County, Minnesota.

    iii.   OLIVER WYMAN FOSTER was born on 05 Jun 1896 in Minnesota. He died on 08 Sep 1959 in Itaska County, Minnesota.

    iv.   CHARLES HENRY FOSTER was born on 13 Jan 1899 in Minnesota. He died on 02 May 1986 in Arizona.

More About Charles Henry Foster:
Living In: 1930 With his parents in Mizpah, Koochiching County, Minnesota.
Occupation: 1930 in Mizpah, Koochiching County, Minnesota; Odd Jobs Laborer

    v.   CHESTER EARL FOSTER was born on 24 Nov 1903 in Minnesota. He died on 30 Nov 1963 in Itaska County, Minnesota.

More About Chester Earl Foster:
Living In: 1930 With his parents in Mizpah, Koochiching County, Minnesota.
Occupation: 1930 in Mizpah, Koochiching County, Minnesota; Odd Jobs Laborer

18. **CHARLES WESLEY**[3] **TUCKER** (William Henry Harrison[2], Henry William[1]) was born on 05 May 1878 in Martinsburg, Knox County, Ohio. He died on 14 Sep 1949 in St. Paul, Ramsey County, Minnesota. He married Mary Karen Sorenson, daughter of Rasmus Sorenson between 05 Jun 1900-13 Jun 1905. She was born about 1882 in Minnesota. She died on 03 Jan 1950 in Bemidji, Beltrami County, Minnesota.

More About Charles Wesley Tucker:
Occupation: 1900 in Bartlett Township, Todd County, Minnesota; Farmer Occupation: 1905 in Bartlett Township, Todd County, Minnesota; Railroad Laborer
Occupation: 1918 in Bemidji, Beltrami County, Minnesota; Brakeman on M&J Railroad
Occupation: 1920 in Bemidji, Beltrami County, Minnesota; Railroad Brakeman

Occupation: 1930 in Bemidji, Beltrami County, Minnesota; Brakeman on Steam Railroad
Occupation: 1940 in Bemidji, Beltrami County, Minnesota; Brakeman on Steam Railroad

Charles Wesley Tucker and Mary Karen Sorenson had the following children:

    i.   ROY[4] TUCKER was born about 1907 in Canada.

    ii.   FLORENCE TUCKER was born about 1909 in Canada.

    iii.   IRENE CONSTANCE TUCKER was born in Jan 1920 in Minnesota.

    iv.   MILTON W. TUCKER was born about 1914 in Minnesota.

    More About Milton W. Tucker:
    Living In: 1940 With his parents in Bemidji, Beltrami County, Minnesota.
    Occupation: 1940 in Bemidji, Beltrami County, Minnesota; Carpenter on Steam Railroad

Generation 4

19. **HUTSON EDWARD**[4] **TUCKER** (Joseph B.[3], Wesley Summers[2], Henry William[1]) was born on 15 Feb 1883 in Perry Township, Hocking County, Ohio. He died on 13 Jul 1945 in Lancaster, Fairfield County, Ohio. He married **LUZELLA (ZELLA) ARTES**. She was born on 10 Jan 1884 in Fairfield County, Ohio. She died on 12 Feb 1930 in Berne Township, Fairfield County, Ohio.

More About Hutson Edward Tucker:
Burial: 16 Jul 1945 in Maple Hill Cemetery, Stoutsville, Fairfield County, Ohio
Cause Of Death: Ruptured Appendix

More About Luzella (Zella) Artes:
Burial: 14 Feb 1930 in Maple Hill Cemetery, Stoutsville, Fairfield County, Ohio

Notes for Luzella (Zella) Artes:
Usually known as "Zella".

Hutson Edward Tucker and Luzella (Zella) Artes had the following children:

    i.   LULA MAE[5] TUCKER was born about 1906.

    ii.   JOSEPH TUCKER was born about 1907.

    iii.   LOYD TUCKER was born about 1909.

20.   **CHARLES JOSEPH**[4] **TUCKER** (Hollis Clark[3], Wesley Summers[2], Henry William[1]) was born on 12 Oct 1879 in Hocking County, Ohio. He died on 13 Jan 1967 in Hocking County, Ohio. He married Beatrice Applegate, daughter of Walter Applegate and Miranda McFarland about 1903. She was born on 08 Mar 1883 in Lancaster, Ohio. She died on 13 Feb 1952 in Hocking County, Ohio.

More About Charles Joseph Tucker:
Living In: 1900 Living with his paternal grandparents in Rockbridge, Goodhope Township, Hocking County, Ohio
Living In: 1910 Goodhope Township, Hocking County, Ohio
Living In: 1920 Franklin, Franklin County, Ohio
Living In: 1930 Columbus, Franklin County, Ohio
Living In: 1940 Columbus, Franklin County, Ohio
Occupation: 1900 in Rockbridge, Good Hope Township, Hocking County, Ohio; Rig Builder

More About Beatrice Applegate:
Burial: 16 Feb 1952 in Sunset Cemetery, Galloway, Franklin County, Ohio

Charles Joseph Tucker and Beatrice Applegate had the following children:

   i.   LOLA PAULINE[5] TUCKER was born on 02 Apr 1904 in Good Hope Township, Hocking County, Ohio. She died on 08 Sep 1989 in Riverside County, California. She married Denver Dayton Painter, son of Henry R. Painter and Margaret Thumb on 30 Jul 1926 in Pickaway County, Ohio. He was born on 19 Apr 1908 in West Virginia. He died on 21 Jun 1990 in Monroe County, Florida.

   ii. WALTER HOLLIS TUCKER was born on 05 Feb 1906 in Rockbridge, Good Hope Township, Hocking County, Ohio. He died on 04 Mar 1971 in Broward County, Florida. He married Dorothy Ely, daughter of John Ely and Stella Long on 24 Dec 1928 in Franklin County, Ohio. She was born on 13 Jan 1907 in Greenfield, Ohio.

   iii. RUDYARD KIPLING TUCKER was born on 04 Jan 1908 in Rockbridge, Hocking County, Ohio. He died on 09 Apr 1926 in Columbus, Franklin County, Ohio.

        More About Rudyard Kipling Tucker:
        Burial: 12 Apr 1926 in Memorial Burial
        Park Occupation: ; Carpenter Apprentice

   iv. MARGARET TUCKER was born on 20 Dec 1909 in Rockbridge, Hocking County, Ohio. She died on 30 Dec 1986 in Palm Beach County, Florida. She married Harold H. Eigensee, son of Charles Eigensee and Emma Borchers on 06 Apr 1933 in Franklin County, Ohio. He was born on 21 Sep 1907 in Columbus, Franklin County, Ohio. He died on 30 Nov 1991 in Upper Arlington, Franklin County, Ohio.

        More About Margaret Tucker:
        Occupation: 1933; Bookkeeper

   v.   KATHRYN TUCKER was born on 13 Feb 1913 in Hocking County, Ohio. She died on 13 Apr 1994 in Mansfield, Richland County, Ohio. She married Nelson Floyd Calendine, son of Alvin Calendine and Evelyn Martin on 31 Aug 1932 in Wayne County, Indiana. He was born on 09 Feb 1912 in Columbus, Franklin County, Ohio. He died on 06 Jun 1973 in Mansfield, Richland County, Ohio.

   vi. RUTH LOUISE TUCKER was born on 05 Nov 1914 in Columbus, Ohio. She died on 24

Jan 1941 in Columbus, Franklin County, Ohio. She married Floyd E. Wright, son of Samuel S. Wright and Frances R. Sharp on 06 Nov 1931 in Richmond, Wayne County, Indiana. He was born on 24 Dec 1905 in North Judson, Indiana. He died on 21 Jul 1979 in Columbus, Franklin County, Ohio.

More About Ruth Louise Tucker:
Burial: 27 Jan 1941 in Memorial Park

vii. BETTY JEAN TUCKER was born on 20 Jun 1921 in Columbus, Franklin County, Ohio. She died on 17 Dec 1997 in Ventura County, California. She married CARL HENRY ALSBERG. He was born on 18 Nov 1919 in Belleville, Essex County, New Jersey. He died on 07 Jul 2013.

viii. CHARLES J. TUCKER was born on 10 Jan 1924 in Franklin County, Ohio. He died on 14 Jun 1944 in Normandy, France.

More About Charles J. Tucker:
Burial: Sunset Cemetery, Galloway, Franklin County, Ohio
Military Service: Bet. 08 Sep 1942-14 Jun 1944 ; World War Two

Notes for Charles J. Tucker:
Government notation on application for a government issued headstone states Charles was serving with Company C, 70th Tank Battalion when he was killed in action. On June 14, 1944 the 70th Tank Battalion was serving in Normandy, France.

----

21. MARY LOVETTA[4] TUCKER (Hollis Clark[3], Wesley Summers[2], Henry William[1]) was born on 17 Aug 1883 in Perry Township, Hocking County, Ohio. She died on 17 Feb 1951 in Salt Creek Township, Hocking County, Ohio. She married William Elmer Woltz, son of Moses H. Woltz and Anna L. Shellhammer on 14 Dec 1901 in Logan, Ohio. He was born on 30 Dec 1880 in Good Hope Township, Hocking County, Ohio. He died in 1955.

More About Mary Lovetta Tucker:
Burial: 20 Feb 1951 in Mount Olive Cemetery, South Perry, Hocking County, Ohio
Cause Of Death: Coronary Thrombosis

Notes for Mary Lovetta Tucker:
Ohio Marriage Records give Rockbridge, Ohio as birthplace of Mary Tucker.

More About William Elmer Woltz:
Burial: Mount Olive Cemetery, South Perry, Hocking County, Ohio
Living In: 1930 Columbus, Franklin County, Ohio
Living In: 1940 Columbus, Franklin County, Ohio
Occupation: 1900 in Good Hope Township, Hocking County, Ohio; Farm Labor
Occupation: 1910 in Pittsburgh, Allegheny County, Pennsylvania; Stationary Engineer
Occupation: 1920 in Youngstown, Mahoning County, Ohio; Railroad Repairman

Notes for William Elmer Woltz:
World War One draft registration has birth date as November 20, 1881.
World War Two draft registration has November 20, 1880 for birth date.

1900 U.S. Census has birth date as November 1883.
Marriage license has November 20, 1881 as birth date.
Birth record has December 30, 1880 for date of birth.

William Elmer Woltz and Mary Lovetta Tucker had the following children:

27.   i. THOMAS ELMER[5] WOLTZ was born on 26 Jun 1902 in Good Hope Township, Hocking County, Ohio. He died on 25 Apr 1936 in Zanesville, Ohio. He married Helen Bluhm, daughter of Frederick Bluhm and Anna Eisennicher on 23 Jul 1923 in Franklin County, Ohio. She was born on 13 Jun 1904 in Columbus, Ohio. She died on 29 Sep 1935 in Columbus, Ohio.

        ii. HOPE DORA WOLTZ was born on 18 Apr 1905 in Rockbridge, Good Hope Township, Hocking County, Ohio. She died on 13 Jan 1993 in Columbus, Franklin County, Ohio. She married (1) RAY P. MEEKS, son of E. H. Meeks and Anna Hingman on 10 Oct 1925 in Franklin County, Ohio. He was born on 22 Jul 1899 in Marion, Virginia. She married (2) RUSSELL JAMES KOST, son of Joseph I. Kost and Caroline Friedly on 23 Jan 1945 in Hocking County, Ohio. He was born on 05 Oct 1905 in Columbus, Ohio. He died on 19 May 1981 in Fairfield County, Ohio.

More About Hope Dora Woltz:
Living In: 1930 Divorced and living with her parents in Columbus, Franklin County, Ohio.
Living In: 1940 Divorced and living with her parents in Columbus, Franklin County, Ohio.
Occupation: 1930 in Columbus, Franklin County, Ohio; Bakery Helper
Occupation: 1940 in Columbus, Franklin County, Ohio; Department Store Saleslady

        iii. YVONNE WOLTZ was born on 15 Aug 1911 in Ohio. She died on 11 Jan 1980 in Broward County, Florida. She married CECIL E. SHACKELFORD. He was born on 10 Jan 1907 in Clarksburg, Harrison County, West Virginia. He died on 01 Mar 1986 in Broward County, Florida.

More About Yvonne Woltz:
Occupation: 1930 in Columbus, Franklin County, Ohio; Restaurant Waitress

22.   **WILLIAM EDWARD[4] TUCKER** (Hollis Clark[3], Wesley Summers[2], Henry William[1]) was born on 08 Nov 1885 in Rockbridge, Ohio. He died on 21 Apr 1975 in Plant City, Florida. He married Mary Ann Davis, daughter of Levi Davis and Mary Ann Bigham on 29 Jun 1906 in Lancaster, Ohio. She was born on 16 Mar 1887 in Laurel Township, Hocking County, Ohio. She died on 11 Mar 1971 in Lakeland, Polk County, Florida.

More About William Edward Tucker:
Burial: Pleasant Grove Cemetery, Durant, Florida
Living In: 1908 Rockbridge, Goodhope Township, Hocking County, Ohio
Living In: 1910 Good Hope Township, Hocking County, Ohio
Occupation: 1920 in Columbus, Franklin County, Ohio; Structural Iron Worker on Bridge Work
Occupation: 1930 in Columbus, Franklin County, Ohio; Iron Worker Building Bridges
Occupation: 1940 in Columbus, Franklin County, Ohio; Iron Worker with Iron Contractor

Notes for William Edward Tucker:
Working as a Union Iron Worker at Jackson Iron and Steel Company, Jackson, Ohio in 1942.

More About Mary Ann Davis:
Burial: Pleasant Grove Cemetery, Durant, Florida
Occupation: School Teacher

William Edward Tucker and Mary Ann Davis had the following children:

28.   i.   WILLIAM HOLLIS[5] TUCKER was born on 28 Jan 1907 in Good Hope Township, Hocking County, Ohio. He died on 13 May 1951 in Nelsonville, Ohio. He married Mazie Ellen Turbett, daughter of Charles Monroe Turbett and Cora Bell Bartley on 02 May 1931 in Franklin County, Ohio. She was born on 10 Feb 1910 in Columbus, Franklin County, Ohio. She died on 11 Jan 1996 in Pickaway County, Ohio.

      ii.   EVLYN MARIE TUCKER was born on 18 Jul 1908 in Millville, Hocking County, Ohio. She died on 19 Mar 1988 in Athens, Athens County, Ohio. She married ARTHUR B. HILT. He was born on 16 May 1916 in Hocking County, Ohio. He died on 07 Jun 1963 in Nelsonville, Athens County, Ohio. She married (2) EARL CHARLES SALTZ, son of Charles Saltz and Laura Yearling on 15 Jun 1931 in Franklin County, Ohio. He was born on 15 Feb 1899 in Columbus, Franklin County, Ohio. He died on 14 May 1971 in Big Spring, Howard County, Texas.

More About Evlyn Marie Tucker:
Burial: Pleasant Grove Cemetery, Durant, Florida
Living In: 1930 With her parents in Columbus, Franklin County, Ohio.
Living In: 1988 Vinton County, Ohio
Occupation: 1930 in Columbus, Franklin County, Ohio; Cutter in Shoe Factory
Military Service: Bet. 29 Aug 1944-10 Jan 1945 in Enlisted July 31, 1944 at Fort Hayes, Columbus, Ohio; U. S. Army, World War Two

Notes for Evlyn Marie Tucker: No Children.

Enlisted in Womens Army Corps at Fort Hayes, Columbus, Ohio on July 31, 1944. Reported for active duty August 29, 1944 at Cleveland, Ohio. Service number A 512 088.

----

29.   iii. PHYLLIS OLENE TUCKER was born on 21 Mar 1922 in Columbus, Ohio. She died on 7 Mar 1991 in Lancaster, Ohio. She married Robert McDaniel Stewart, son of Van Robert Stewart and Elsie Myrtle Casto on 27 Sep 1940 in Logan, Hocking County, Ohio. He was born on 17 Dec 1920 in Mason County, West Virginia. He died on 18 Jul 1977 in Plant City, Florida.

23.   DAVID WESLEY[4] TUCKER (Hollis Clark[3], Wesley Summers[2], Henry William[1]) was born on 28 Jun 1894 in Rockbridge, Hocking County, Ohio. He died on 25 Feb 1984 in Fairfield County, Ohio. He married Minnie Turner, daughter of Martin Turner and Harriet Fuller on 06 Jan 1923 in Pickaway, Ohio. She was born on 08 Jul 1901 in New Holland, Pickaway County, Ohio. She died on 16 Jan 1987 in Lancaster, Ohio.

More About David Wesley Tucker:
Burial: Fairview Methodist Church Cemetery, Good Hope Township, Hocking County, Ohio
Living In: 1920 With his mother in Goodhope Township, Hocking County, Ohio.
Living In: 1984 in Hocking County, Ohio
Occupation: 1910 in Goodhope Township, Hocking County, Ohio; Newsboy
Occupation: 1920 in Goodhope Township, Hocking County, Ohio; Tool Presser for Oil Company

Occupation: 1930 in Goodhope Township, Hocking County, Ohio; Public School Teacher
Occupation: 1940 in Goodhope Township, Hocking County, Ohio; Teacher at Private High School

More About Minnie Turner:
Burial: Fairview Methodist Church Cemetery, Good Hope Township, Hocking County, Ohio

Notes for Minnie Turner:
Social Security death index gives date of birth as July 8, 1901. Ohio death index has date of birth as 1902.

David Wesley Tucker and Minnie Turner had the following children:

    i.   DAVID W.[5] TUCKER was born on 23 Feb 1924 in Hocking County, Ohio. He died on 02 Nov 1984 in Logan, Hocking County, Ohio. He married Hester Sharon on 17 Jul 1973 in Hocking County, Ohio. She was born on 21 Apr 1926 in Adams County, Ohio. She died on 11 Mar 2000 in Lancaster, Fairfield County, Ohio.

        More About David W. Tucker:
        Burial: Fairview Methodist Church Cemetery, Good Hope Township, Hocking County, Ohio
        Living In: 1984 Rockbridge, Hocking County, Ohio
        Military Service: S2, U.S. Navy, World War Two

    ii.   HELEN HULS TUCKER was born on 10 Sep 1925 in Rockbridge, Ohio. She died on 29 Nov 2010 in Logan, Ohio.

        More About Helen Huls Tucker:
        Burial: 02 Dec 2010 in Fairview Methodist Church Cemetery, Good Hope Township, Hocking County, Ohio

        Notes for Helen Huls Tucker:
        Logan: Helen Huls Tucker 85, of Logan, Ohio passed away Monday, November 29, 2010, at Creatview Nursing Home, Lancaster, Ohio.

        Helen was born September 10, 1925, in Rockbridge, Ohio to David W. Tucker Sr. and Minnie Tucker.

        She was a 1942 graduate of Rockbridge High School; graduate of Ohio OSU with a bachelors in business administration; member of Mensa: worked 37 years for IBM in White Plains, New York and Columbus, Ohio: and was a member of the Avent Christian Church of Rockbridge, Ohio.

        Surviving are sister, Doris (Paul) Seymour of Lancaster, Ohio; brother, John Martin Tucker of Lancaster, Ohio; and nieces and nephews..

        Helen was preceded in death by her parents; and brothers, David W. Tucker Jr. and Larry Eugene Tucker.

        Funeral services will be held at 11 a.m. Thursday, December 2, 2010 at the Heinlein-Brown Funeral Home, Logan, Ohio, with the Rev. Diora Edgell officiating.

        Burial will be at Fairview Cemetery, Rockbridge, Ohio. Calling hours will be observed Wednesday, December 1, 2010 from 5 to 8 p.m. at the funeral home.

----

    iii.   DORIS IRENETUCKER was born on 10 Aug 1926 in Hocking County, Ohio. She married Paul Emerson Seymour, son of Thomas Seymour and Ethel Wagner on 29 Jun 1945 in Meigs County, Ohio. He was born on 06 Feb 1924 in Circleville, Pickaway County, Ohio. He died on 05 Apr 2007 in Lancaster, Fairfield County, Ohio.

    iv.

More About Doris IreneTucker:
Occupation: 1945 in Cheshire, Meigs County, Ohio; Secretary

    v.   JOHN MARTIN TUCKER was born about 1928 in Ohio.

    vi.   LARRY EUGENE TUCKER was born on 21 Jan 1930 in Rockbridge, Hocking County, Ohio. He died on 23 Jan 1930 in Good Hope Township, Hocking County, Ohio.

More About Larry Eugene Tucker:
Cause Of Death: Premature Birth

24.   **BERTHA MAY**[4] **TUCKER** (Hollis Clark[3], Wesley Summers[2], Henry William[1]) was born on 31 Mar 1896 in Millville, Hocking County, Ohio. She died on 30 Nov 1973 in Hocking County, Ohio. She married Clyde Mathias, son of William Mathias and Laura Hixon on 26 Sep 1922 in Hocking County, Ohio. He was born on 16 May 1897 in Lancaster, Ohio. He died on 05 Oct 1964 in Athens, Athens County, Ohio.

More About Bertha May Tucker:
Living In: 1920 With her mother in Goodhope Township, Hocking County, Ohio
Occupation: 1920 in Goodhope Township, Hocking County, Ohio; Public School Teacher
Occupation: 1922 in Rockbridge, Hocking County, Ohio; Teacher

More About Clyde Mathias:
Burial: Fairview Methodist Church Cemetery, Hocking County, Ohio
Occupation: 1920 in Good Hope Township, Hocking County, Ohio; Pipe Line Labor
Occupation: 1922 in Warren, Ohio; Steel Worker
Occupation: 1930 in Good Hope Township, Hocking County, Ohio; Pipe Puller on Gas Wells
Occupation: 1940 in Rockbridge, Hocking County, Ohio; Pipe Puller with Own Shop
Military Service: Bet. 24 Sep-11 Dec 1918 ; Company C, 380th Infantry, U.S. Army

Clyde Mathias and Bertha May Tucker had the following children:

    i.   WILLIAM H.[5] MATHIAS was born on 19 Feb 1924 in Rockbridge, Hocking County, Ohio. He died on 03 Jun 1997 in Lancaster, Fairfield County, Ohio. He married Clara Orville Dusenbery, daughter of Guy Dusenbery and Anna Furniss on 25 Nov 1948 in Hocking County, Ohio. She was born on 07 Oct 1929 in Delaware County, Ohio. She died on 21 Jan 2001 in Lancaster, Fairfield County, Ohio.

More About William H. Mathias:
Military Service: U. S. Navy

    ii.   ROBERT CLYDE MATHIAS was born on 16 May 1927 in Ohio. He died on 30 Jan 2006 in Lancaster, Fairfield County, Ohio. He married FRANCES HEWITT. She was born in 1932.

More About Robert Clyde Mathias:
Burial: Forest Rose Cemetery, Lancaster, Fairfield County, Ohio
Military Service: U. S. Navy

25. **BERYL HOLLIS**[4] **TUCKER** (Hollis Clark[3], Wesley Summers[2], Henry William[1]) was born on 19 Aug 1902 in Rockbridge, Hocking County, Ohio. He died on 11 Sep 1983 in Hocking County, Ohio. He married Ruth Irene Primmer, daughter of William Primmer and Blanche A. Starner on 01 Jan 1927 in Hocking County, Ohio. She was born on 17 Apr 1908 in Rockbridge, Hocking County, Ohio. She died on 18 Sep 2006 in Lancaster, Fairfield County, Ohio.

More About Beryl Hollis Tucker:
Burial: Fairview Methodist Church Cemetery, Good Hope Township, Hocking County, Ohio
Occupation: 1930 in Good Hope Township, Hocking County, Ohio; Mail Carrier on Mail Route
Occupation: 1940 in Good Hope Township, Hocking County, Ohio; Rural Letter Carrier

Notes for Beryl Hollis Tucker:
Birth record gives his name as Hollis Beryl Tucker. Marriage license gives his name as Beryl H. Tucker. Ohio death index gives his name as Beryl H. Tucker. Headstone has Beryl Hollis Tucker.

More About Ruth Irene Primmer:
Burial: 22 Sep 2006 in Fairview Methodist Church Cemetery, Good Hope Township, Hocking County, Ohio
Living In: 2006 Hocking County, Ohio

Notes for Ruth Irene Primmer:
Ruth Irene Tucker

     ROCKBRIDGE - Ruth Irene Tucker, 98, of Rockbridge, Ohio departed this earthly life Monday, Sept. 18, 2006, at Fairfield Medical Center in Lancaster, Ohio.
     Mrs. Tucker was born April 17, 1908, in Rockbridge, to Blanche Starner Primmer and William Primmer. She was preceded in death by her husband, Beryl Hollis Tucker.
     She was a graduate of Rockbridge High School, where she was valedictorian and played basketball. At the time of her death she was the oldest surviving member of the class of 1927.
     A lifelong and devoted member of Rockbridge Advent Christian Church, she served over the years as a Sunday school teacher, superintendent of the Sunday school, delegate to the annual conference, and as a member of the Helper's Union.
     Mrs. Tucker played the piano well and had a beautiful singing voice. Her children and grandchildren especially loved to hear her sing, "My Grandfather's Clock," "Because He Didn't Think," and "Bill Terrell," a song that she learned in grade school about the murder of a girl in Logan.
     Surviving are her sons, Don Eugene Tucker, of Kitty Hawk, N.C., Roger Alyn Tucker of Somonauk, Ill., and Stanley Keith Tucker of Newark, Ill.; her sisters, Helen Beougher, Geraldine Leohner, and Rhea McKown; her grandchildren, Janet, Kerry, Richard, Trisha, Kristin, Anita, Brian, and Sheri; and her great-grandchildren, Wesley, Owen, Jamie, and Jordan.
     She was preceded in death by her husband and their sons Larry and Danny.
     Calling hours are 6 to 9 p.m. Thursday, Sept. 21, at Heinlein Brown Funeral Home in Logan, Ohio, and one hour prior to the service at the church.
     The funeral service is Friday, Sept. 22 at 3 p.m. at Rockbridge Advent Christian Church in Rockbridge with Pastor David Woodyard and Pastor Diora Edgell officiating.

Beryl Hollis Tucker and Ruth Irene Primmer had the following children:

i.   DONALD EUGENE[5] TUCKER was born on 03 Feb 1928 in Ohio. He married ELIZABETH (UNKNOWN).

ii.   LARRY BERYL TUCKER was born on 01 Nov 1931 in Ohio. He died on 01 Mar 1982 in Guernsey County, Ohio.

     More About Larry Beryl Tucker:
     Burial: Fairview Methodist Church Cemetery, Good Hope Township, Hocking County, Ohio
     Living In: 1982 Rockbridge, Hocking County, Ohio

iii.   DANIEL D. TUCKER was born on 03 Oct 1936 in Rockbridge, Hocking County, Ohio. He died on 21 Aug 2005 in West Lafayette, Coshocton County, Ohio. He married LINDA (UNKNOWN).

     More About Daniel D. Tucker:
     Burial: 25 Aug 2005 in Memory Gardens, Coshocton, Coshocton County, Ohio Military Service: SP4, U.S. Army

     Notes for Daniel D. Tucker:
           Coshocton Tribune
     WEST LAFAYETTE - Daniel D. Tucker, 68, of West Lafayette, passed away Sunday, Aug. 21, 2005, at his residence.

     He was born Oct. 3, 1936, in Rockbridge, to Ruth (Primmer) Tucker of Rockbridge and the late Beryl Tucker.

     He was a graduate of Rockbridge High School and received his Bachelor of Science from Aurora College, Aurora, Ill. and his Masters Degree in Science from Ohio University. He taught general science and biology for over 30 years at Ridgewood High School, and was an advisor for Future Teachers of America and the Yearbook Annual. He was a former member of the West Lafayette Lions Club and Newcomerstown Elks, and was a member of the West Lafayette United Methodist Church, where he was a delegate to its annual conference for several years. He also served in the U.S. Army.

     He is survived by a daughter, Anita J. Tucker of Cleveland; former wife, Linda Tucker of West Lafayette; and three brothers, Don (Elizabeth) Tucker of Kitty Hawk, N.C., Roger Tucker of Somonauk, Ill., and S. Keith (Norma) Tucker of Newark, Ill.

     He was preceded in death by a brother, Larry Tucker.

     The funeral will be at 11 a.m. Thursday, Aug. 25, at the West Lafayette United Methodist Church, with the Rev. James Woodring officiating. Burial will be at Coshocton County Memory Gardens.

     Calling hours will be from 6 to 8 p.m. Wednesday, Aug. 24, at Given-Dawson, Coshocton, Funeral Home, and one hour prior to service at the church Thursday.
----

iv.   ROGER ALYN TUCKER was born on 09 Jun 1938 in Ohio.

v.   STANLEY KEITH TUCKER was born on 03 Dec 1940 in Ohio. He married Norma Nell Johnson, daughter of Joseph Johnson on 31 Aug 1963 in Augusta, Georgia.

26.   **NORMA IRENE**[4] **TUCKER** (Hollis Clark[3], Wesley Summers[2], Henry William[1]) was born on 27 Mar 1905 in Rockbridge, Hocking County, Ohio. She died on 21 May 1985 in Lancaster, Fairfield County, Ohio. She married Ernest Loy Fauble, son of Chris Fauble and Eliza J. (Jennie) Dupler on 24 Dec 1926 in Hocking County, Ohio. He was born on 06 Sep 1904 in Rockbridge, Hocking County, Ohio. He died on 27 Jan 1967 in Lancaster, Fairfield County, Ohio.

More About Norma Irene Tucker:
Burial: Maple Grove Cemetery, Lancaster, Fairfield County, Ohio

Notes for Norma Irene Tucker:
Birth record gives her name as Norma Irene Tucker but she was usually known as Irene. Ohio death index has her name as Norma I. Fauble. Social Security death index has her name as Irene Fauble.

More About Ernest Loy Fauble:
Burial: Maple Grove Cemetery, Lancaster, Fairfield County, Ohio
Occupation: 1930 in Lancaster, Fairfield County, Ohio; Foundry Foreman
Occupation: 1940 in Lancaster, Fairfield County, Ohio; Government Mail Man

Ernest Loy Fauble and Norma Irene Tucker had the following children:

i.   EVELYN M.[5] FAUBLE was born on 27 Nov 1928 in Fairfield County, Ohio. She married Raymond Eugene Shull, son of Frank H. Shull and Lucy G. Krile on 14 Aug 1951 in Fairfield County, Ohio. He was born on 27 Nov 1924 in Fairfield County, Ohio. He died on 06 Apr 2008.

More About Evelyn M. Fauble:
Occupation: 1951 in Lancaster, Fairfield County, Ohio; Office Worker

ii.   LOIS J. FAUBLE was born on 22 Jan 1932 in Lancaster, Fairfield County, Ohio. She died on 31 Jul 2008 in Columbus, Franklin County, Ohio. She married Warren Edison Martin, son of Merrill H. Martin and Georgia M. Black on 16 Dec 1951 in Fairfield County, Ohio. He was born on 07 May 1930 in Lancaster, Fairfield County, Ohio. He died on 06 Jun 2006 in Franklin County, Ohio.

More About Lois J. Fauble:
Burial: Forest Hills Memory Gardens, Lancaster, Fairfield County, Ohio
Occupation: 1951 in Lancaster, Fairfield County, Ohio; Clerk

Notes for Lois J. Fauble:
Lois Martin, 76, passed away Thursday, July 31, 2008, at Mt. Carmel East Hospital.

We, your family, love you very much. We believe you're the best grandma and mother in the whole world. Thanks for being the best. When you meet God, put in a good word for us. Life might change us, but we start and end with family. Tell grandpa and Mary Sue hello.

She is survived by three beautiful children, Laura, Tim and Karen; four "grands", Alex, Nicole, Tim and Rob; sisters, Evelyn Shull and Nancy Eyman; and brother,

Earl Fauble.

She was precede indeath by he husband, Warren Martin; and parents, Ernest and Irene Fauble.

She was retired elementary school teacher with Columbus Public Schools.

Lois was an amazing quilter and proudly displayed he quilts throughout her home. She was a proud member of theGillie Recreation Center, where she joined other avid quilters.

A Celebration of Life Service will take place Sunday at her home. Schoedinger Northeast Chapel is entrusted with her arrangements.

Originally published in the Lancaster Eagle Gazette August 2, 2008

----

   iii.   EARL LOY FAUBLE was born on 09 May 1934 in Ohio.

Generation 5

27.   THOMAS ELMER[5] WOLTZ (Mary Lovetta[4] Tucker, Hollis Clark[3] Tucker, Wesley Summers[2] Tucker, Henry William[1] Tucker) was born on 26 Jun 1902 in Good Hope Township, Hocking County, Ohio. He died on 25 Apr 1936 in Zanesville, Ohio. He married Helen Bluhm, daughter of Frederick Bluhm and Anna Eisennicher on 23 Jul 1923 in Franklin County, Ohio. She was born on 13 Jun 1904 in Columbus, Ohio. She died on 29 Sep 1935 in Columbus, Ohio.

More About Thomas Elmer Woltz:
Burial: 28 Apr 1936 in Memorial Burial Park, Muskingum County, Ohio
Cause Of Death: Pulmonary Occlusion
Occupation: Steel Constructor

Notes for Thomas Elmer Woltz:
Ohio Birth Index gives name as Moses Elmer Woltz. 1910 U.S. census gives name as Moses E. Woltz. 1920 U.S. census gives name as Thomas Woltz. Death certificate gives first name as Tom. Wife's death certificate gives his name as Thomas E. Marriage license gives name as Thomas.

More About Helen Bluhm:
Burial: 02 Oct 1935 in Memorial Burial Park

Thomas Elmer Woltz and Helen Bluhm had the following children:
   i.   MARY F.[6] WOLTZ was born about 1924 in Ohio.

      More About Mary F. Woltz:
      Living In: 1940 With her paternal grandparents in Columbus, Franklin County, Ohio.

   ii.   JOANN WOLTZ was born about 1929 in Ohio.

      More About Joann Woltz:
      Living In: 1940 With her paternal grandparents in Columbus, Franklin County, Ohio.

iii.   BILLIE L. WOLTZ was born about 1931 in Ohio.

More About Billie L. Woltz:
Living In: 1940 With her paternal grandparents in Columbus, Franklin County, Ohio.

iv.   ELMER WOLTZ was born about 1934 in Ohio.

More About Elmer Woltz:
Living In: 1940 With his paternal grandparents in Columbus, Franklin County, Ohio.

28.   **WILLIAM HOLLIS[5] TUCKER** (William Edward[4], Hollis Clark[3], Wesley Summers[2], Henry William[1]) was born on 28 Jan 1907 in Good Hope Township, Hocking County, Ohio. He died on 13 May 1951 in Nelsonville, Ohio. He married Mazie Ellen Turbett, daughter of Charles Monroe Turbett and Cora Bell Bartley on 02 May 1931 in Franklin County, Ohio. She was born on 10 Feb 1910 in Columbus, Franklin County, Ohio. She died on 11 Jan 1996 in Pickaway County, Ohio.

More About William Hollis Tucker:
Burial: 16 May 1951 in Mount Olive Cemetery, South Perry, Hocking County, Ohio
Cause Of Death: Coronary Thrombosis
Living In: 1930 With his parents in Columbus, Franklin County, Ohio.
Occupation: 1930 in Columbus, Franklin County, Ohio; Iron Worker Building Bridges
Occupation: 1931 in Franklin County, Ohio; Painter
Occupation: Magician
Military Service: Company D, 29th Engineer Battalion, U.S. Army, World War Two

Notes for William Hollis Tucker:
Served in Company D, 29th Engineer Battalion, U.S. Army, World War Two.

More About Mazie Ellen Turbett:
Burial: Mount Olive Cemetery, South Perry, Hocking County, Ohio

William Hollis Tucker and Mazie Ellen Turbett had the following children:

30.   i. HOLLIS DAVIS[6] TUCKER was born on 27 Jan 1933 in Ohio. He died on 09 May 1984 in Palm Beach County, Florida. He married ARLENE (UNKNOWN).

ii. CHARLES EDWARD TUCKER was born on 29 Jul 1937 in Ohio. He died on 19 Apr 1980 in Franklin County, Ohio. He married MIRIUM (UNKNOWN).

More About Charles Edward Tucker:
Burial: Mount Olive Cemetery, South Perry, Hocking County, Ohio
Military Service: Bet. 01 Nov 1954-25 Nov 1955 ; U.S. Air Force

31.   iii. ARTHUR LEE TUCKER was born on 24 Aug 1943 in Columbus, Ohio. He died on 27 May 2009 in Ashville, Ohio. He married BELINDA (UNKNOWN).

32.   iv. CAROLYN SUE TUCKER. She married DARRELL GRIFFITH.

29.   **PHYLLIS OLENE[5] TUCKER** (William Edward[4], Hollis Clark[3], Wesley Summers[2], Henry William[1]) was

born on 21 Mar 1922 in Columbus, Ohio. She died on 07 Mar 1991 in Lancaster, Ohio. She married Robert McDaniel Stewart, son of Van Robert Stewart and Elsie Myrtle Casto on 27 Sep 1940 in Logan, Hocking County, Ohio. He was born on 17 Dec 1920 in Mason County, West Virginia. He died on 18 Jul 1977 in Plant City, Florida.

More About Phyllis Olene Tucker:
Burial: 11 Mar 1991 in New Fairview Cemetery, Logan, Ohio

More About Robert McDaniel Stewart:
Burial: 21 Jul 1977 in Pleasant Grove Cemetery, Durant,
Florida
Living In: 1935 Toledo, Lucas County, Ohio
Occupation: 1938 in Hocking County, Ohio; Working in Electrical Refrigeration
Occupation: Apr 1940 in Logan, Hocking County, Ohio; Cab Driver for Cab Company
Occupation: Sep 1940 in South Perry, Hocking County, Ohio; Bar Tender

Robert McDaniel Stewart and Phyllis Olene Tucker had the following children:

33.   i. MARY SANDRA[6] STEWART was born on 17 Nov 1942 in Columbus, Ohio. She married HARRY DAVENPORT. She married HAROLD OATES.

34.   ii. EVLYN MARIE STEWART was born on 17 Dec 1944 in South Perry, Ohio. She married FRANKLIN EUGENE TIMMS. He was born on 03 May 1940 in Dundas, Ohio.

    iii. JON ROBERT STEWART was born on 15 Dec 1947 in Logan, Ohio. He died on 17 Dec 1947 in Logan, Ohio.

More About Jon Robert Stewart:
Burial: 18 Dec 1947 in Smith Chapel Cemetery, Logan, Hocking County, Ohio Cause Of Death: Premature

Notes for Jon Robert Stewart:
Buried with his paternal grandparents.

35.   iv. HOPE ELLEN STEWART was born on 27 Jun 1949 in South Perry, Ohio. She married David Garland Edwards on 09 Mar 1968 in Tampa, Florida. He was born on 21 May 1945 in Fort Sumner, New Mexico.

Generation 6

30.   HOLLIS DAVIS[6] TUCKER (William Hollis[5], William Edward[4], Hollis Clark[3], Wesley Summers[2], Henry William[1]) was born on 27 Jan 1933 in Ohio. He died on 09 May 1984 in Palm Beach County, Florida. He married ARLENE (UNKNOWN).

Hollis Davis Tucker and Arlene (unknown) had the following children:
    i. DAWN[7] TUCKER.

    ii. MARK TUCKER.

    iii. LISA TUCKER.

31.   ARTHUR LEE[6] TUCKER (William Hollis[5], William Edward[4], Hollis Clark[3], Wesley Summers[2], Henry William[1]) was born on 24 Aug 1943 in Columbus, Ohio. He died on 27 May 2009 in Ashville, Ohio. He married BELINDA (UNKNOWN).

More About Arthur Lee Tucker:
Burial: Mount Olive Cemetery, South Perry, Hocking County, Ohio
Cause Of Death: Lung Cancer
Military Service: United States Air Force

Arthur Lee Tucker and Belinda (unknown) had the following children:

    i.   REBEKAH[7] TUCKER. She married (UNKNOWN) COPELAND.

    ii.   PATRICIA TUCKER.

    iii.   JAMES TUCKER.

    iv.   JOHN TUCKER.

    v.   JENNIFER TUCKER. She married (UNKNOWN) MEAD.

    vi.   BENJAMIN TUCKER.

32.   **CAROLYN SUE**[6] **TUCKER** (William Hollis[5], William Edward[4], Hollis Clark[3], Wesley Summers[2], Henry William[1]). She married **DARRELL GRIFFITH**.

Darrell Griffith and Carolyn Sue Tucker had the following children:

    i.   MARY SUE[7] GRIFFITH.

    ii.   DARRELL RUSSELL GRIFFITH.

33.   **MARY SANDRA**[6] **STEWART** (Phyllis Olene[5] Tucker, William Edward[4] Tucker, Hollis Clark[3] Tucker, Wesley Summers[2] Tucker, Henry William[1] Tucker) was born on 17 Nov 1942 in Columbus, Ohio. She married **HARRY DAVENPORT**. She married **HAROLD OATES**.

Harry Davenport and Mary Sandra Stewart had the following children:

    i.   PHYLLIS[7] DAVENPORT.

37.   ii.   PEGGY DAVENPORT.

    iii.   GENA DAVENPORT.

    iv.   DAVID DAVENPORT.

Harold Oates and Mary Sandra Stewart had the following child:

37.   i.   TIMOTHY ROBERT[7] OATES was born on 20 Oct 1960. He married DEANNA (UNKNOWN).

34.   **EVLYN MARIE**[6] **STEWART** (Phyllis Olene[5] Tucker, William Edward[4] Tucker, Hollis Clark[3] Tucker, Wesley Summers[2] Tucker, Henry William[1] Tucker) was born on 17 Dec 1944 in South Perry, Ohio. She married **FRANKLIN EUGENE TIMMS**. He was born on 03 May 1940 in Dundas, Ohio.

Franklin Eugene Timms and Evlyn Marie Stewart had the following children:

38.   i.   ROBERT[7] TIMMS. He married RENEE WOMELDORF.

39.   ii.   JOHN MARTIN TIMMS was born on 04 Jan 1965 in Lancaster, Ohio. He married TOBBI ELLEN TAYLOR. She was born on 11 Jan 1963 in Sacramento, California.

35. HOPE ELLEN[6] STEWART (Phyllis Olene[5] Tucker, William Edward[4] Tucker, Hollis Clark[3] Tucker, Wesley Summers[2] Tucker, Henry William[1] Tucker) was born on 27 Jun 1949 in South Perry, Ohio. She married David Garland Edwards on 09 Mar 1968 in Tampa, Florida. He was born on 21 May 1945 in Fort Sumner, New Mexico.

David Garland Edwards and Hope Ellen Stewart had the following children:

40. i. DIANA GAIL[7] EDWARDS was born on 28 Mar 1969 in Plant City, Florida. She married Mark Gregory Simmons on 23 Dec 1988 in Plant City, Florida.

41. ii. DARLENE MARIE EDWARDS was born on 28 Dec 1970 in Plant City, Florida. She married Randall Edward Thompson on 12 Sep 1993 in Pickerington, Ohio.

iii. PATRICIA ANNE EDWARDS was born on 20 Oct 1972 in Plant City, Florida. She died on 20 Oct 1972 in Plant City, Florida.

More About Patricia Anne Edwards:
Burial: Pleasant Grove Cemetery, Durant, Florida

Generation 7

36. PEGGY[7] DAVENPORT (Mary Sandra[6] Stewart, Phyllis Olene[5] Tucker, William Edward[4] Tucker, Hollis Clark[3] Tucker, Wesley Summers[2] Tucker, Henry William[1] Tucker, Harry).
Peggy Davenport had the following child:

i. ALEX[8] DAVENPORT.

37. TIMOTHY ROBERT[7] OATES (Mary Sandra[6] Stewart, Phyllis Olene[5] Tucker, William Edward[4] Tucker, Hollis Clark[3] Tucker, Wesley Summers[2] Tucker, Henry William[1] Tucker) was born on 20 Oct 1960. He married DEANNA (UNKNOWN).

Timothy Robert Oates and Deanna (unknown) had the following children:

i. MCKENZIE[8] OATES.

ii. SANDRA OATES.

iii. TIMOTHY OATES.

38. ROBERT[7] TIMMS (Evlyn Marie[6] Stewart, Phyllis Olene[5] Tucker, William Edward[4] Tucker, Hollis Clark[3] Tucker, Wesley Summers[2] Tucker, Henry William[1] Tucker, Franklin Eugene, John Martin, Charles Vance, Ezra Quimby, Richard, John B.). He married RENEE WOMELDORF.

Robert Timms and Renee Womeldorf had the following children:

i. DANIELLE[8] TIMMS.

ii. CASSANDRA TIMMS.

iii. ROBERT RYAN TIMMS.

39. JOHN MARTIN[7] TIMMS (Evlyn Marie[6] Stewart, Phyllis Olene[5] Tucker, William Edward[4] Tucker, Hollis Clark[3] Tucker, Wesley Summers[2] Tucker, Henry William[1] Tucker) was born on 04 Jan 1965 in Lancaster, Ohio. He married TOBBI ELLEN TAYLOR. She was born on 11 Jan 1963 in Sacramento, California.

John Martin Timms and Tobbi Ellen Taylor had the following children:

i.   IAN CONNER[8] TIMMS was born on 20 Mar 1992 in Chillicothe, Ohio.

ii.   MARY KATHERINE TAYLOR TIMMS was born on 30 Mar 1998 in Chillicothe, Ohio.

40.   **DIANA GAIL**[7] **EDWARDS** (Hope Ellen[6] Stewart, Phyllis Olene[5] Tucker, William Edward[4] Tucker, Hollis Clark[3] Tucker, Wesley Summers[2] Tucker, Henry William[1] Tucker) was born on 28 Mar 1969 in Plant City, Florida. She married Mark Gregory Simmons on 23 Dec 1988 in Plant City, Florida.

Mark Gregory Simmons and Diana Gail Edwards had the following children:

i.   MARK GREGORY[8] EDWARDS was born on 20 Jun 1988 in Plant City, Florida. He married Julie Ann Mercer on 17 Feb 2007 in Wellston, Ohio. She was born on 28 May 1988.

ii.   DAVIAN GAIL SIMMONS was born on 12 Feb 1991 in Monroe, North Carolina.

41.   **DARLENE MARIE**[7] **EDWARDS** (Hope Ellen[6] Stewart, Phyllis Olene[5] Tucker, William Edward[4] Tucker, Hollis Clark[3] Tucker, Wesley Summers[2] Tucker, Henry William[1] Tucker) was born on 28 Dec 1970 in Plant City, Florida. She married Randall Edward Thompson on 12 Sep 1993 in Pickerington, Ohio.

Randall Edward Thompson and Darlene Marie Edwards had the following children:

i.   TREVOR[8] THOMPSON was born on 11 Sep 1995.

ii.   VICTORIA KATHLEEN THOMPSON was born in Mar 1997.